NEW WRITING / BOOK TALK / NEWS AND REVIEWS

THE READER

No. 44 WINTER 2011

Published by The Reader Organisation at The University of Liverpool.
Supported by:

the reader
organisation

UNIVERSITY OF
LIVERPOOL

EDITOR   Philip Davis

DEPUTY EDITOR   Sarah Coley
CO-EDITORS   Maura Kennedy
                          Angela Macmillan
                          Eleanor McCann
                          Brian Nellist

ADDRESS   The Reader Magazine
                          The Reader Organisation
                          The Friary Centre
                          Bute Street
                          Liverpool
                          L5 3LA

EMAIL   magazine@thereader.org.uk
WEBSITE   www.thereader.org.uk
BLOG   www.thereaderonline.co.uk

DISTRIBUTION   See p. 128

ISBN 978-0-9567862-3-4

SUBMISSIONS

The Reader genuinely welcomes submissions of poetry, fiction, essays, readings and thought. We publish professional writers and absolute beginners. Send your manuscript with SAE please to:

The Reader Organisation, The Friary Centre, Bute Street, Liverpool, L5 3LA

Printed and bound in the European Union by Bell and Bain Ltd, Glasgow

NEWS AND EVENTS

GET INTO READING EXPANDS in LONDON

This autumn, our Get Into Reading project has expanded its reach in London: we now have Reader-in-Residences in Tower Hamlets, Lambeth and Kensington & Chelsea, delivering weekly, read aloud groups across a variety of sectors: primary health care, mental health, libraries and community organisations.

VOLUNTEER READING SCHEME

We have won over £400,000 for a five-year volunteer reading scheme on Merseyside. Funded by the Big Lottery, this flagship volunteer project seeks to enable those at risk of or suffering from mental health difficulties, isolation or unemployment to benefit from joining a team of volunteers who will take our weekly Get Into Reading groups to elderly people in care homes on Merseyside.

A LITTLE, ALOUD

Sales of *A Little Aloud* reached 11335 this summer and are still going strong. Thank you to everyone who's already bought the book and remember, with Christmas just around the corner, it makes a perfect present. Visit www.alittlealoud.com to leave your comments about your reading experience

EVENTS – PENNY READINGS

The **Penny Readings**, our all-singing, all-dancing reading extravaganza takes place in Liverpool's St George's Hall on Sunday 4th December at 6pm, with special guest reader David Morrissey. **The Ha'penny Readings**, an event just for young people aged 8–16, returns for a second year too, held on the same day at 2.30pm with author Tommy Donbavand.

In January 2012, **Penny Readings** go to London, celebrating the start of Dickens' bicentenary year with a fantastic ensemble of writers, musicians, magicians and very special readers. We're hosting the event with Vintage Books at the British Library on 22nd January at 2.30pm. Visit our website for more information about how to get tickets to these events: www.thereader.or.guk/penny-readings.

CONTENTS

THE READER'S
PENNY
READINGS

LIVERPOOL
DECEMBER 4
(ST GEORGE'S HALL)

&

LONDON
22 JANUARY
(BRITISH LIBRARY)

EDITORIAL

ON GUSTO

Philip Davis

W hat would you like now?' I asked him after the main course was finished. 'More roast potatoes and some Bach,' was our guest's reply. 'The beginning of the *St. Matthew Passion*. And no extra greens, thank you, but a drop more wine.'

Don't we like the people who know what they want? When I was younger I used to be the polite and backward sort who always wanted to be asked twice. 'No, I couldn't possibly'... 'Oh go on with you – just a little?'...'Okay then, well, thank you.' I hate that tone of satisfaction by pretend defeat, and such apologies for desire are not just to do with what goes on at the table. If you are going to sin, sin boldly! said Martin Luther. The latter-day Lutheran at our Sunday-lunch table had a direct and unashamed *appetite* for life at sundry levels, and preferably those sundry levels all at the self-same time.

The Romantic essayist, William Hazlitt called it the gusto of life. To him it meant, for example, not only seeing a painting but feeling it. The very skin in the colouring of a Titian gives, he says, that sort of *tingling* sensation to the eye, which the body feels within itself. Gusto is what happens when the eye has imagination, when the eye:

acquires a taste or appetite for what it sees. In a word, gusto in painting is where the impression made on one sense excites by affinity those of another.

Spuds go in at the mouth and Bach goes in through the ear.

There is a sort of plucky defiance, a rude health about gusto. I remember years ago the critic George Steiner coming to a conference we held in Liverpool. As Steiner moved towards risky territory, the chairman of his session, one of the then great and good, Sir Roy Shaw of the Arts Council, hastily intervened to say that we should not be dealing on this occasion in matters of religion or politics. 'Thus,' said Steiner in unabashed delight, 'our esteemed Chair has sought to purge our discussion of two of the major concerns of human life.' Then he went on regardless of course to speak of God and Marx and other of his familiars. I don't recall, though, George being a great eater or drinker, at least of the fare we were able to offer him.

I like my own wine flavoured with the pinch of sadness –and this in accordance with Mr Hazlitt's recipe that calls for the richest blend of all our senses together. As we move into 2012 and the bicentenary of the birth of Dickens, that great man of gusto, what about this, then, from *Bleak House*? One character is telling another of the interminable goings-on in the Court of Chancery. And what is the best laugh, practically the only joke, that ever comes up in that dreary and pointless travesty of justice? It is when a sorry figure regularly gets up to plead his own hopeless case – the appellant known familiarly and for years throughout the court as The Man From Shropshire. Then there is a pause. '*I*,' says this speaker, passionately beating one hand in the palm of the other, '*I* am the man from Shropshire . . .'

Only a few months later, finally worn out by it all, the man from Shropshire lies on his death bed. The policeman who customarily arrests him for protest and disruption stands disconsolate at the bedside. Come on, sir – he goads and urges – let's go back to my chasing you and you evading arrest. That is what we are both used to: it is our way of life, our game. Worn-out: surely not worn-out? says the alarmed policeman, for so long the formal antagonist but now speaking from somewhere else disguised within that continuing role:

> **'Now I tell you what *you* want. You want excitement, you know, to keep you up; that's what you want. You're used to it, and you can't do without it. I couldn't myself. Very well, then; here's this warrant. What do you say to coming along with me, and having a good angry argument before the Magistrates. It'll do you good, it'll freshen you up. You're half the fun of the fair in the Court of Chancery.'**

It is no good this time – which is the sign of its being the last time. But the idea that we can and must make life out of anything, involuntarily giving the passion of gusto even to the sufferings we have had to get used to – that pays some tribute to the inventiveness of the sheer human desire to live as long and as well as possible. It makes me think of a friend telling me over lunch how the dying often seem to wait till family are out of the room in order to slip away. Or of the couple who decided, in the midst of caring for their stricken second child, to have a third, against all external advice, to make the family more. Or the bereaved one forgetting loss for a moment in all the triviality of some bargain found in the shops. These things also gather around a book as its other senses, from other places.

And I think too of Scrooge at this Christmas time, finally repenting his meanness towards Bob Cratchit, whom he has so long ill-treated. It is not done – do you remember? – in pious apology, in guilt and shame and speechifying, but in a gusto which the wonderful Alastair Sim caught so magnificently in the classic film of 1951 (and I wish there was a biography of him).

Instead, just at this last minute Scrooge continues in character, one more time in his old bad character, before leaving it for ever. It is the farewell performance of what before had seemed so permanently twisted; a celebratory demonstration of this sudden about-change. For now on the morning after Christmas

Day, Bob is a little late, in fact eighteen minutes-and-a-half late, as his employer reckons it. What right have you to be late? What do you mean by having enjoyed yourself last night or in being sorry now? 'I am not going to stand this thing any longer,' roars Scrooge, till Bob thinks Scrooge is going to beat or fine or sack him, even on this day:

> **'And therefore I am about to RAISE your salary... A merry Christmas, Bob!' said Scrooge with an earnestness that could not be mistaken, as he clapped him on the back. 'A merrier Christmas, my good fellow, than I have given you, for many a year.'**

That little touch 'merrier' is so subtle – in its tacit admission of a regret that still must not spoil the relished improvement. There are no mistakes left in these great disguises through which we share a truer understanding – the new will emerging out of the old appearances, the bad tone making a joke of a good thing, the sad life redeemed by the gusto that won't give up within it.

Eat well, sin boldly, and stir yourself up. A Happy Christmas to all our Readers.

EDITOR'S PICKS

Jeanette Winterson talks with Jane Davis about her recently published memoir *Why Be Happy When You Could Be Normal?* – the title comes from the question asked by her adoptive mother when, aged sixteen, Jeanette fell in love with a woman and left home. In this interview she talks movingly about the book's main concerns, her suicidal breakdown and the search for her birth mother that followed. The interview is interspersed with extracts from the book.

Peter Robinson and **Julie-ann Rowell** feature amongst our poets, while **Kate Miller** is the latest to take us behind the scenes of her poems in 'Poet on her Work'.

In fiction, **Gabriel Josipovici** gives us a Christmas story with a twist, while in 'Shine' **B. J. Epstein** writes a modern Cinderella story. Keeping up the festive spirit **Ian McMillan** takes us back to his early Christmases. To help parents and all of our readers with young friends, we recommend seasonal books for children of all ages.

Our essays offer a diverse assortment of subjects with **Brigid Lowe Crawford** on her reasons for taking time out to raise her family, **Malcolm Bennett** on ear wax, and **Alan Wall** continuing his series on the oddities of language. **Anna Lawrence Pietroni** recommends the difficulties of one of *The Reader*'s favourites, Russell Hoban's *Riddley Walker.*

FACE TO FACE

MEET THE POET

**JULIE-
ANN
ROWELL**
on p.32

Favourite place in the world

My favourite place in the world is India, though it is a complex choice. My first visit was to Mumbai and it was overwhelming: the sheer number of people, the colours, smells, noise, elephants strolling between traffic, the traffic! The extraordinary juxtaposition of extreme poverty and extreme wealth. Nothing hidden. My partner and I became film stars walking along Juhu beach, constantly stopped to pose for photographs and video. But soon we learnt how to be part of the scenery. There is a way, though it is hard to explain unless you have been to India.

Favourite place in the world

Our bedroom in Reading. It's a small room with the double bed filling about half of it, facing the back window, across which is a slatted blind not taken by the previous owner. My side is the left, with a Japanese bookshelf against the wall behind the door, and another book-filled open-shelved cupboard beside it. The view is across our brie-shaped allotment strip to an alley, sheds, the backs of terraces opposite, their roof-lines, chimneys, trees, and sky. I like to lie there as the sun comes up, and our local world emerges from darkness. It's an inspiration.

**PETER
ROBINSON**
on p.43

Longest gestation period for a poem?

'Winter Sleep', took a long time – eight or so years. It began with an unusually clear dream: a girl of three or four years old arrived at my door and told me she'd travelled from Central Asia (where my father had his origins). Several years later I dreamt of her again: she said she was my daughter and that now, aged ten, she spoke many languages. More years passed and one evening (I was recollecting Little Venice where I'd worked light years before) I found myself writing. In an hour or so 'Winter Sleep' took shape fairly quickly. I wish I could be that patient as a rule!

GILL
GREGORY
on p.59

GORDON
SCAPENS
on p.78

Should your poems be read silently or aloud?

I prefer my poems to be read silently. A person reading aloud would be aware of others around, maybe an audience, and would be concerned with pronunciation and voice control to the detriment of concentration. A poem read silently blots out everything else. The reader has the chance to stand in another's shoes, relate the words to his own life. The poem should be read several times, each time something more being revealed.

Which poet would you like to have met?

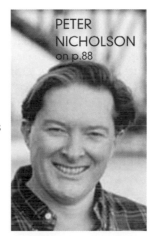

PETER
NICHOLSON
on p.88

Without doubt Emily Dickinson. Which means I would not have met her as she was notoriously reclusive. I think she is the greatest of the American poets, along with Whitman. She is passionate, intelligent and cogent and writes to the depth of herself and to the depth of Thou. Surely it is time for a film about this writer. The Coen brothers? Why Emily? Her wildness, her atom-splitter energies, her lyric intensity, her celebration of beauty. Put simply, her greatness.

KATE MILLER

THE POET ON HER WORK

ON 'NEREID WITH SEABIRD'

Kate Miller

Nereid With Seabird

I
Guide to Xanthos

A salamander, poker-length,
slumps off its bed of carved oak-leaves
abandoned in the dust.

We're hailed by an ancient mariner
wind-dried and skinny as a mullein spike,
his language like the Lycian blocks

turned upside-down, texts
cut and added to in Greek.
His German's botched with English

for a speech about a siege. He mimes
the way the city's population died.
They set themselves on fire and leapt

from rocks, their burning bodies
raining on the beach of the Esen,
pale green and thin beneath.

He knows nothing of a bridge or avenue
to link the fabled port, the sacred ponds
and precinct of Letoon

to Xanthos. Once it might have led us
to the feet of Leto's handmaids
placed to greet us on the temple

celebrating victory,
a troupe of dancers, lovely and unruly,
gracing the façade towards the sea.

My uncle used to say
they seemed to flurry in from bathing,
shaking off seawater.

Ankle to chin, wet
skin and almost see-through silks
like showgirls' flashed.

One he picked out as different,
more of a child still
acquiring grown-up grace.

She didn't strike a pose or try
to tame her spraying skirts.
She had to run to keep

her balance while the gull
she stood on rode the breeze.
That's how he always spoke of her – as real.

STATUE FROM THE NEREID MONUMENT

DRAWING BY JAN REEVES
IN CHALK AND INDIAN INK

II
At the British Museum – The Last Visit

Today before I neared the usual room, a child ran up,
             stopped short, teetered
    about a metre off,
on tiptoe – in periwinkle shoes – put out
his arms as if to reach a rail
                or steady oars to keep
          himself afloat. Just as a water-boatman
     on the pond makes skeeterings,
so he made rings
         in air, force-fields that spun
about his outstretched hands and new found feet.
Those little shoes were beautiful. The stone
     he skated on was light.

Watch me, he gestured, *I am so alive!*

     while I'm the one who doesn't move.
For years I've gone along to see a broken thing
          of stone, and sat too often over-hot
    like any visitor in hospital,
distracted by illuminated signs,
        the clock, attendants.

          Who will be the first to move?
She's no more disfigured, deaf,
       fixed in one place than I am.
     From now on, let her run to me
       hooped in her cloak,
          arriving like the child
             full of life.

      We'll greet each other with the same delight.

Late October, early November is always a productive time of the year for my writing, a result, I think, of losing the light, marking the close of another year of growth and maturation. Several years back, I dashed down a clutch of poems that celebrated a long relationship I'd been conducting in the British Museum. Since that Autumn I have mulled over and rebuilt them as a sequence, twinning pairs together, adding two completely new poems, (the first, a marriage of old drafts with new fieldwork, now opens the sequence) published here. Early versions were extended from notes in a Moleskine and sketchbook I kept while I was a student of Jo Shapcott, attending classes in Bedford Square. I'd take a shortcut through the museum (warm and dry), which coincided nicely with the assignment: describe your Muse. Assuming you have one ... but if not, where better to look for such a thing?

Once, as researcher for an art encyclopaedia, I had to assemble out-of-copyright illustrations of artists' workshop practice. This entailed hours in the British Library Reading Room, housed until 1997 in the rotunda at the British Museum. When it came to techniques of sculpture, I took advice from sculptors and restorers working now. Tools and methods have changed little in millennia, they said, and since the BM contains fabulous evidence of the extraordinary life of stone fashioned into images, which you are permitted to photograph, look there for evidence. Often as not, the sculptures are still standing in the same spot and in the same light as I first clapped eyes on them. Perhaps exactly as my grandmother saw them forty years previously?

Picture-research completed, I kept returning to the Nereid Monument from Lycia (Mediterranean Turkey). You pass it before you reach the Parthenon marbles. What it lacks in fame, male torsoes and gods, it makes up for in whirling girl figures, whose real significance to the governor of Xanthos, who commissioned them, is not revealed. My diary records 'facing running girl... echoes across stone floor' on 31 October, 2005, one of six headless figures displayed alongside friezes and ruined fragments. The catalogue shows parts of many others. I became fixed on 'Nereid with Seabird' at her feet, apparently skimming waves, singled out in 'Guide to Xanthos', as the one, my 'uncle used to say' was 'different, more of a child still acquiring grown up grace'.

You could say it's not a 'she', not a girl, just a large damaged piece of stone. The figure is draped in fine wet cloth, naturally sticking to her skin, giving the strong impression that it is see-through. But there really is no clinging fabric, merely the sense of a covering, which to the touch would be inert and unyielding. Everything is marble. If you step behind the piece, the carving of the flying cloak and base is left rough, where marks of the point – a big pointed tool like a vast pencil – and broad chisel are visible, unrefined, unpolished. Behind one knee, lightly carved creases in her damp skirt are like the shallow grooves of pencilled lines following the contours. You see, not a grubby block of stone with bits cut and smashed from it, but a tender study of a girl's body in rapid movement. It is what sculpture can do and cryogenics can't, freeze a living form without taking life out of it. This enduring sign of life is over two thousand years old.

Sculpture exercises a force-field that draws me, physically engaging me as if by a magnetic charge, equally powerful from little shapes like the archaic Cycladic dolls or Inuit whalebone carvings as from these great figures. I think it must be because small objects bear so many traces of handling, turning, being used for ritual and storytelling. And big ones seem to carry energy from their places of origin into our present day experience. Richard Jefferies, nature writer, tells in *The Story of My Heart* (1883) how he visits the BM to get a sense of landscape, escaping from his city office to breathe properly, feel the sun that once warmed the sculptures release him from cold and discomfort. (He was to die of tuberculosis soon after completing his quite mystical autobiography). I let the idea form that the stone figure healed in the dark and that, sealed in after visiting hours, a watcher would learn from seeing that happen. It raised many problems of representation. From my notes: 'poem must be a little theatre, a cyclorama or black box with a light trained on the subject – but you can't fly off the stage with her, too elastic, too mobile – you can't take the audience into the darkness with your actor.' In 2006, I outlined this aspect of the 'Muse' poem. Under the title 'Girl Running Still' it bore an epigraph from John Berger: 'The relationship between what we see and what we know is never settled.'

Aspects of realisation, of moving between real and unreal, started to affect and shape the many subsequent revisions and the eventual sequence. The cluster of early poems that followed in Autumn 2006 were patched in with research about Xanthos, once a great Lycian city, now a World Heritage site, close to the temple complex of Letoon, in the froggy, marshy delta of the Xanthus river (present day Esen). There are nineteenth century engravings of the ruined site when archaeologists under Sir Charles Fellowes crated up the good pieces to send to London. But it was impossible to imagine the dramatic impact of the temple front built in 390BC. To make it real, I decided, I must go to Xanthos. I had imagined, for example, storks in that landscape. But were there?

Before I could travel to Turkey I tried to discover from notes, drawings and curling photographs – still pinned on my study wall as I write – what was at the heart of the obsession with the 'broken thing of stone'. Lifting my encounter with a small boy – flying 'like a small plane' in the creamy light of the Great Court – I wrote 'The Visit' in January 2008, from a typed stream of consciousness, where I found a slightly sinister foreboding about what else happens in 'the usual room':

in a room with ugly tiles and thick grout, a hospital vestibule place, she tries to come after me out of her stoniness, a body, disfigured, heavy and so old, tries to wrest my attention. It's the pull.

Now 'The Last Visit', it comes second in the sequence, and appears here with a spirited drawing by Jan Reeves, that really conveys the animation of the carved girl, not her amputations. The more I recall the gloomy and grotesque institutional feel of a museum with its mortuary significance, the sadder it makes me! By repeatedly visiting the Nereid, I cautiously began to acknowledge that I was responding to her as if she were a person I'd known, or more mysteriously would come to know. As I've grown older I realise 'she' meant both child and ancestor to me. I think of my grandmother reminiscing how, when I was born, my father returned from sea that morning and telephoned to say he going to see the baby, so excited he hadn't stopped to ask whether it was girl or boy. What mattered was his delight in becoming a father, having a child. Perhaps some of that has crept into 'Last Visit'.

As for the uncle, I borrowed him. I was at a supper party on Millennium Eve sitting beside an art historian more passionate than I am about figure sculpture. Recently he led a group of friends to Xanthos and taught them all he knew about the Nereids. I wish I had been there. He is the ideal 'guide to Xanthos'. (Not the flawed but comic guide who mimes, in the opening poem, ancient citizens valiantly going to their deaths at the end of a disastrous siege). The uncle I dreamed up was outside time; he could have been in Lycia when the temple was unveiled. Undoubtedly he responds to the eroticism in the group of girls, each dancer carved by a different, inevitably male hand, each trying to catch your eye by her (meaning *his* skill in rendering) body-language. If I have taken liberties with my sources it is because they are many and unexpected in their connections. I agree with Elizabeth Bishop who, replying to questions about where her poems come from, wrote that

it takes an infinite number of things coming together, forgotten, or almost forgotten, books, last night's dream, experiences past and present – to make a poem. The settings or descriptions of my poems are almost invariably just plain facts – or as close to the facts as I can write them.

Places where something starts – and the peculiar pilgrimages to find those places, and re-visit them once found – have been a recurring preoccupation for these five years. I have been writing about places of origin without knowing at the start what I was after. Oh yes, storks nest near Xanthos, recorded in my diary, July 2008, perched on a wheel above an orchard of fat plums. I shall be on my way back there as this goes to print.

FICTION

CHRISTMAS

Gabriel Josipovici

Frank, the father, is waiting at the station.

– What's all this? he says.

– Don't worry, the son says. I haven't come to stay.

– I didn't think for a moment that you had, the father says. I was just –

– Careful! It's fragile.

– What is it?

– You'll see.

He gets into the passenger seat and the father starts the car. – You're looking well, he says.

– Am I?

– In the circumstances.

– Yeah.

Frank has not known his son so silent. – How's Timothy? he asks.

– Shit Dad, his son says. Don't make conversation.

– I just asked.

– OK.

They are silent until he pulls into the drive and brings the car to a stop. They get out.

– No, his son says, I'll handle it. It's delicate.

GABRIEL JOSIPOVICI

READING AT SHAKESPEARE & CO IN PARIS

– What is it?

– Nothing. I'll show you later.

– I'm intrigued.

– It's just something I'm making for Tim.

– What sort of thing?

– Oh, a Noah's Ark.

– A Noah's Ark? What are you talking about?

– It's a school project.

– A Noah's Ark?

– Uhuh.

The father leads the way. - I've put you in your old room, he says. Or would you rather have the usual?

– Whatever.

Now he can see his son in a good light he finds he isn't looking all that well after all.

– I just thought you wouldn't want the double bedroom now you...

– Whatever, his son says.

– I thought it might bring back memories and...

– Don't be so damned sensitive, his son says. And then go on about it.

They stand in the doorway of the small bedroom.

– So that I'll say: sensitive! his son says angrily.

– I'm sorry, he says. Your mother always stopped me. She kept me from making a fool of myself.

– Oh, Dad, for God's sake! his son says. Just get out of the room and let me unpack.

– Sorry.

– Just get out, Dad, his son says. Just get out.

* * *

– Hey! the son says as he comes into the kitchen. A fire. Great!

– I thought we could eat in here, Frank says. I don't use the dining room much any more.

– I like it here, the son says. It feels good.

– We always had a fire in here, Frank says. When your mother was alive. Do you remember?

25

– It's great, the son says. I've brought you some single malt, he says, putting the bottle down on the kitchen table.

– I don't drink any more.

– You don't? Why not?

– I'm afraid.

– What of?

– That I might not be able to stop. Now I'm by myself.

– Oh, come off it, Dad, his son says.

– I've cooked something nice for us this evening.

– That's good. Mind if I have a glass?

– Of course not. Do you want something with it?

But his son has already opened the bottle.

– Ice? Frank says. Water?

– No no, his son says.

They sit at the kitchen table.

After a while his son says: – You don't want to see it?

– What?

– The Noah's Ark.

– Of course. Bring it down.

– It's a bit big. You come and see it.

They climb the stairs.

– Is the room all right? the father asks.

– Of course. Why?

– I don't know. Your mother dealt with all that sort of thing.

– What sort of thing?

– Allotting rooms to guests. Making beds and so forth.

– It's not very difficult, is it?

– No. But I was afraid I might have forgotten something. So, he says, squatting down on the floor to get a closer look. This is it.

– It's a project, the son says. They all have to make something.

– Why are you doing it for him then?

– I'm not doing it. I'm only helping. It's his idea and everything.

– So they don't all have to do an ark?

– No no. Whatever they want.

– What gave him the idea?

– He likes animals.

– There aren't any animals.

– They're too difficult to do and then fit in. This is the ark before the animals came in.

– I see, Frank says.

– He likes boats too.

– I know Frank says.

– I thought it might be because it was the first bit of carpentry and all that, he says after a while.

– What do you mean?

– It's in the Bible.

– I know it's in the Bible!

– I mean no-one except God ever made anything before that.

– Really?

– Why did you bring it down with you? Frank asks.

– I still have a few things to do to it. And I thought if I had time I might start painting it.

– You're painting it?

– Yes. Why not? A nice red. Make it stand out.

– Red?

– Why not?

– I don't know. I thought… Do you want to use the garage?

– The garage?

– To paint it?

– Can we go downstairs? his son says. When's dinner? I'm hungry.

– It's almost ready. It's pretty basic. Your mother did all the cooking.

– For God's sake, Dad! his son says. She's been dead three years.

– What difference does that make?

– Don't go on about it! his son says.

* * *

The son reaches across the table and pulls the bottle of wine to him.

– Sorry, Frank says. Help yourself.

– I still can't believe it, his son says. I still don't know what happened.

The father is silent.

– I know she still loves me, his son says. I can hear it in her voice on the phone.

– Give her time, Frank says.

– Time! his son says. She's living with this guy. She's chosen him over me. I can't believe it.

He pours himself another glass of wine.

– These things happen, his father says.

– I didn't think they'd happen to me.

– You haven't met anyone else? his father asks

– Dad, the son says. I love her. She loves me. It doesn't make any sense.

– We've got to play the cards we're dealt, his father says. Look at me.

– Shit, Dad, the son says. You're old. Mother was old. She died. She loved you. How can you compare the two things?

– I'm not comparing, his father says. I wouldn't compare a death to a marital problem.

– Fuck you, Dad, his son says. You insist I come down for Christmas, and then you give me this shit? Is there another bottle somewhere?

– I thought we should be together at a time like this, his father says, getting up to fetch another bottle. Families should stick together at Christmas.

– Here, give it to me, his son says, taking the bottle and corkscrew from him.

He pours himself another glass. – I try to hate her, he says. For what she's done to me. To Tim. But I can't. I love her, Dad. And I know she loves me too, only she's got this thing into her head and…

– Give her time, his father says. She'll come back.

– I don't want her back, the son says. Not after what she's done to me.

– Then what do you want?

– I want to die, his son says.

His father is silent, staring at him across the table.

He gets up and clears away the plates. – Shall we keep the Christmas pudding till tomorrow? he asks.

– Whatever, his son says.

– Perhaps we'd better, the father says.

– Whatever, the son says.

– It's a difficult time, the father says. The darkest time of the year. That's why families get together and everyone eats as much as they can, isn't it? You'll feel better as soon as the days start getting longer.

– You know what I did last summer? his son says. After she left? I never even drew the curtains. I couldn't stand all that light and the thought of everybody else having a good time. I couldn't stand it.

The father is silent.

– I'd rather kill myself than have another summer like the last, the son says

– Don't talk like that.

– How do you want me to talk then? You and Mum always taught me to speak openly about what I felt. And now I'm doing so you try to shut me up.

– I'm not trying to shut you up, the father says. I just feel such talk is pointless. You only talk yourself into a depression.

– I'm not depressed, his son says, filling his glass again. I just can't see why I should live any more. I can't face twenty-four hours every day and sixty minutes to the hour and sixty seconds to the minute. I see her all the time. I see her with this guy and I see her with me and I hear her voice calling as she used to do when she got home. That's all, Dad. Do you understand? That's all.

– It's supposed to be a time of hope, his father says. The birth of the Christ child and all that.

His son is silent.

– You've got Tim to worry about, so stop being so self-centred, he says.

– That's rich, the son says. That's rich, coming from you.

– What do you mean? Frank says.

His son drains his glass and refills it.

– The trouble with you, his father says, is that we gave you too much love. Now you expect the same from everyone. But you can't get it. Life's not like that. She probably couldn't stand things any more with you, for whatever reason. These things aren't rational, you know. She just felt she had to leave.

– We loved each other, the son says. What there was between us was something I haven't seen among any of the couples I know. I understood her. I understood what made her tick. And she understood me, Dad. It doesn't make sense. Is there another bottle of this?

– Don't you think we should go to bed? his father says.

– And do what? his son says.

The father is silent. Then he says: – You're eaten up with self-pity.

– Perhaps I am, his son says.

The father suddenly feels a rush of love for his son. He gets up and goes round the table. He puts his arms round his shoulders.

– Oh, Dad, stop it, the son says, squirming.

– It'll be all right, Frank says. Whatever happens it'll be all right.

His son pushes his arm away and pours himself another drink.

– I think I'll turn in now, he says.

– Do that, Frank says. Try and get a good night's sleep.

– I've got things to do, his son says. I'm not going to sleep.

– What things?

– Things, his son says. He gets up from the table and weaves his way to the door.

– I thought we might have a walk tomorrow, his father says. Get over to the cliffs.

– Goodbye Dad, his son says, turning at the door.

– Goodnight, Frank says.

* * *

He sits on at the table, listening to his son padding about in the room above. The afternoon and evening have taken it out of him and he finds himself sinking into a doze, still at the table. Finally he hears his son fall heavily on the bed and after that there is a silence.

Turned from the table, he gazes into the fire.

And then he hears it. Plip plip plip plip. He realises he's been hearing it for some time. At once it comes to him. It's drops. On the carpet. He looks up at the ceiling.

A red spot, blotchy, of uneven outline, is clearly visible half-way between the light bulb and the wall. As he watches he sees a red drop form and then slowly detach itself and fall with the now expected noise onto the carpet. Even as it does so another drop has formed and followed it, and then another and another.

Hardly able to breathe, clutching his heart, the father stares at the mark on the ceiling. – Oh God! he says.

He stumbles to the door and climbs the stairs. His legs are so heavy he has to drag himself up by clinging to the banisters. He is aware of how silent the house suddenly is.

On the landing he steadies himself, then pushes open the door of his son's room.

His son is lying, fully clothed, on the bed, one foot still on the floor. The sound of his snores fills the room.

On the floor, by the little wooden boat, a tin of red paint is lying on its side, slowly disgorging its contents onto the carpet.

– Oh God! the father whispers. Oh God! You bastard! You absolute fucking bastard!

'Christmas' originally published in *Heart's Wings: New and Selected Stories*, Carcanet, 2010.

POETRY

JULIE-ANN ROWELL

Crossing

A train crossing in the dark is a chain of eyes,
and, thinking it alive, I yearn to be on board
seeing out from the inside, flickering light an augury
willing me away. I resent standing here in the yard,
air punctured by the low bull push of the throats of frogs
that started on cue when night fell, and the neighbours
have gone to bed, so I'm left with this –

flash-flash, gone-gone, lives moved on, the something
about a train and wanting to be carried, destination certain,
reachable: Baton Rouge, Lafayette. Some people record
identification plates, take photographs, but it's night-time trains
for me, the albino snake of them, the ironic invisible grumbling:
you're left behind, you're left behind, you're left behind.

Indra at Land's End,
Mumbai

I was burning on the promenade
when Indra appeared to me, no glaze
of sweat on *his* wide forehead, and
for a moment he looked fierce, even
without a sword, or hook or anything
I might usually recognise him by. I glanced
away, but he would not be ignored, carrying
a shoe-cleaning box, his dark face
adorned with a leaking eye, his dusty soles
bare, his precious jacket torn,
graceful in his twisting walk. I wanted
to pray to him for thunderous rain to
put a lid on the heat that came
everywhere with me, but then he was only
a shoe-man with his box of tricks, raising
his hand to stop me, in a quest for five rupees.
He turned into a god again when I said no,
summoning his chariot of gold from the sun.

ESSAY

MAMAN DE JOUR

TRUE CONFESSIONS OF A WOMAN OUT OF THE GAME

Brigid Lowe Crawford

The other day I got chatting with another mother, as our children made a den together under a slide. She lived in New York, but I wished she lived next door: we got on like a house on fire. But then came an awkward moment... The Question:
'Do you work... outside the home?'

I launched into an unnecessarily detailed account of my personal circumstances. I told her how I had been on a research contract since the birth of baby number one, and that by turning down teaching, accepting help from family, and doing a lot of work at night, I hadn't needed to send her to nursery. I explained about husband's long working hours, and that since birth of baby number two and the end of my research contract, I hadn't felt able to go back into the job market. I touched, vaguely, on recent freelance writing projects. Finishing my spiel, and taking breath, I was relieved to see she looked sympathetic.

I asked about her own situation. After the birth of her first child she anticipated that number two would follow quickly, and so hadn't been back to work since. But number two was now three-years-old, so she clearly wasn't in a hurry to return.

She sounded apologetic, and I wished I had sounded less so myself. Why the long self-justification, I asked myself?

I feel that my choice is both unusual and controversial. But am I right? About one in nine mothers does not work outside the home. But many children with a parent at home full-time live in households where no-one was working even before children came along. The proportion of women leaving a career to look after children is much smaller. I don't know one academic woman of my generation who has done what I've chosen to do. Apparently, around forty percent of mothers think it a good idea for one parent to stay at home full time with preschool children. But I suspect that approval for stay-at-home parents varies with socioeconomic group too, because it doesn't feel like four in ten in the circles I move in.

But it's the negative attitude of men that has been most striking. I don't know one mother who has felt pressurised by her partner to stay at home with the children, but I know several who have been flatly forbidden to do so. One female friend's partner was alarmed that she might want to emulate my choice. Making it clear that he would never countenance the economic losses involved, he also suggested that it was unhealthy for a woman to give up her independence, and that children looked after by their mothers instead of in nursery would grow up weird and incur bullying at school. Another close friend's partner, whom I also count as a friend of my own, said my choice was 'wrong', that I owed it to society to do the 'highest' sort of work of which I was capable, and that I had no right to squander my time doing work that anyone could do. I haven't heard such unequivocal moral judgment over a 'lifestyle choice' in years – these days people scarcely write off devil worship with such assurance.

Paradoxically, these men seem emboldened by an ostensibly feminist rhetoric to dictate the course of women's lives. Implicit in their arguments is the view that to care for your own children represents a betrayal of other women. I know women who feel this way too and who cite the struggles of their own mothers to win the right to an independent career as the main reason not to compromise their commitment to their own.

Feminism has focused almost exclusively on securing equal rights for women in the world of work outside the home, and work caring for children does get in the way of this objective. The stubborn and sizeable pay-gap between men and women isn't really about gender, it's about mothering: the gap between men and childless women is tiny. The easiest way to eliminate the pay-gap, and to boost GDP in the process, is to discourage women from putting time into (their own) children. So government talks about mothers at home as a 'problem', and when they talk about protecting women's 'choice', really mean subsidising all the childcare options except families caring for their own children at home. Given that staying home was already the most costly option for mothers anyway, this makes most of them feel they have no choice at all. Research confirms that most mothers return to work simply because they can't afford to stay home.

The financial cost of my own choice is very large – the long hours my husband can work because I do most of the parenting has earned him a salary at the bottom of the higher tax bracket, high enough to lose us thousands of pounds of child benefit and tax credits that we would still get if we both earned £40,000 and had almost twice the net income. There is no state help to compensate economically for the loss of my salary. Few other developed countries stack the odds against single-income families to this degree, yet there are no really powerful UK or-ganisations focused on understanding, rewarding or facilitating the work that women do in caring for their own children. The women who write about mothers' choices are mostly women who work, and are therefore focused on defending their own decision. Nevertheless, I have been surprised how many people don't believe that a woman who's been through nine uncomfort-able months of pregnancy has earned the right to care for her own baby.

My male friend's argument that I had a duty to be doing a 'higher' sort of work left me speechless. My perspective is so different that it seemed almost impossible that we could ever understand each other. Before even turning to the issue of childcare, I find it hard to sympathise with his certainty about the ultimate value of his own work. Like me, he's a humanities academic. Don't get me wrong... I quite often, maybe half the time, feel confident that when I write about literature I help unlock something of real value to individuals and societies. In more quixotic moods, I even think that contributing to a body of academic knowledge has a second-order value in itself, as part of a quest for truth that's important for a mature culture. I feel particularly cocksure about all this on those rare occasions when I publish something likely to be read by more people than I could fit in my car.

Nevertheless, I don't lose sleep worrying about the human consequences of my not writing about literature for a few years. On the other hand, when, distracted by the mental effort of grappling with the literary conventions of the *buildungsroman*, or the like, I catch myself looking through, rather than at, my daughter's bright face as she tries to tell me something 'amazing', I do feel a pang. At these times I take to heart afresh the cautionary tale of the scholar Casaubon, who, 'With his taper stuck before him... forgot the absence of windows, and in bitter manuscript remarks on other men's notions about the solar deities [became] indifferent to the sunlight.' The value of the time I spend on my children doesn't have to be wrung painfully out of theories: it's as clear as day.

The decision to stay at home with the children is no more altruistic than going outside on a sunny day. But which of us hasn't felt a dull sense of regret, very like guilt, after missing fleeting hours of sunshine while watching TV indoors?

Looking after children all day builds on and builds up a deep sense of existential perspective. Most careers do exactly the opposite. No matter how much you enjoy your work, the long working hours and continual deadlines force you to get your head down. Once yoked, there's never the opportunity to lift your head and look around, take stock of what you're doing and reflect on its worth to you, and to the rest of the universe.

There is a cruel conflict too between the momentum of a typical professional career and that of female biology. Many women in academia find that by the time they have their degrees, have traversed the wilderness of odd jobs and have finally secured both a reputation and a permanent position, they are of exactly the age when they would like to focus on family. This holds for other careers too. One fantastically talented friend spent her early graduate years as a cleaner, moved up through secretarial jobs, and was recently offered a senior tutorship at an Oxbridge College. Though the job was ideal and the pay wonderful, she was in painful doubt whether to accept. Here, at long last, was a position worth giving her all for, just at a time when she was thinking about turning her energies to having babies. She took the job, but still fears she may have made the personal choices ahead more difficult by doing so. Research shows an increasing number of women swept away by the flow of work, and either spending less time with their children than they would like, or missing the moment for starting a family altogether. Looking out from the world of work, there never seems a good moment to have children.

There's overwhelming evidence that my own career prospects will be badly damaged by a child-rearing break. From most employers' points of view, this is wasted time: I will have gained no skills, and those I did have will be badly rusted.

If I were hiring I would take the opposite view. Research shows that the neural networks of new mothers undergo a growth spurt, and that's certainly what it feels like. In comparison to mother-me, my childless self was workshy, con-ventional, diffident, tentative, childish and slow-moving. My competence, stamina and imagination haven't grown so quickly since I was a child myself. During my years of taking care of the children while at the same time researching, my efficiency and work-rate soared. Tasks took a fraction of the time they used to. Oh, and the worry that putting a career on hold can damage your confidence? As you can see, in my case that's not a problem – though I do have stay-at-home friends whose confidences has been bashed by being constantly referred to as someone 'who doesn't do anything'.

I'm always baffled by the conventional talk about mothers 'vegetating' at home. I do know, and sympathise with, mothers who feel genuinely unhappy spending all day as carers, and ask myself why my own experience has been so different.

One reason must be that I have great family and friend support. Isolation and loneliness can be mistaken for or cause lack of intellectual stimulation. I have a friend who gave up a till job at ASDA, who describes the psychological problems of staying at home with a baby in exactly the same terms as other friends pausing from high-powered careers. But though some mothers at home are genuinely prone to depression, it seems evolutionarily unlikely that looking after children is inherently depressing. It's being at home alone with babies for nine hours or more a day that's hard to bear. A generation ago many families included three generations, so a mother often had relatives at home for help and company. This is seldom the case now. And of course, there are also fewer other non working parents around with whom one might share mental and physical resources.

Maybe loneliness renders mechanical an experience that, well supported, can feel like the most ambitious research project, the most challenging initiative, imaginable. I haven't been as stretched by my most talented Oxbridge students as I have by my growing children. I'm not sure Alan Turing could have broken the code behind the enigma of a one-year-old's night wakings, or whether Einstein could have effectively explained base ten to a student who insisted on playing the violin 'just quietly' at the same time. And could either of them have worked on both problems at once? Answering the questions young children ask helps one understand the world better oneself, and renews mental agility. This morning I've explained democracy, canal locks, why a bike stays upright, and why food cools when you blow on it – all from first principles, but using engaging concrete illustrations. At the same time, I've been trying to follow the lisping, badger-related arguments of a chubby little person who has learnt a dozen new words and a couple of new grammatical constructions since breakfast. A perfect day, lacking only in a spare minute to vegetate.

If I'm going to make new people – and someone has to – I have a duty to make good ones – functional, capable, happy ones. From an economic perspective, the World Bank estimates that three quarters of the man-made (or, in this case, mainly woman-made) wealth of developed countries is embodied in human capital. Evidence confirms the intuition that the more well-educated, attentive and loving a child's carer, the better. I don't know anyone prepared to look after my children who's better qualified than I am, so it seems to me that if I can do it, and enjoy doing it, I should.

But, the world says, kids are resilient and will 'turn out' fine whatever their early experiences. Research suggests that depends on what you mean by 'fine'. And for me, that's beside the point anyway. How children 'turn out' is no more important than the richness of their experience right now. I can't see childhood as a mere training ground for adulthood. Children's capacity for happiness and misery, as well as for imagination, innovation and learning, is greater, not less, than that of adults, as anyone who remembers childhood can testify. Children also create more inspiration, happiness and misery for the people who love them than most adults can. If making children happy isn't a valid end in itself, then I don't know what all our carefully calibrated utilitarian means could possibly be orientated towards. As long as my children and I enjoy exploring together in the sunny morning of their lives, I'll reckon my time well spent.

YOUR RECOMMENDATIONS

RECENT READS

- *The Philosophical Baby* by Alison Gopnik. An amusing exploration of the latest research on the growth of the mind, synthesised into a startlingly new and moving appreciation of childhood.
- *Landing Light* by Don Paterson. An intimate, intense balance between hasty humour and collected Zen.
- The Palliser novels, by Anthony Trollope. In a reversal of my teenage reading habits, these days I skip the young lovers and focus on the humane exploration of political ambition and integrity, the ethics of the press and of coalition government.
- *Mothers and Others: The Evolutionary Origins of Mutual Understanding*, by Sarah Blaffer Hardy. A revolutionary re-framing of the evidence about what made and makes us human.
- *The Egoist*, George Meredith. The most underrated Victorian novel – hilarious, compulsive, and strangely modern.

Brigid Lowe Crawford

- *Elizabeth Bishop and the New Yorker: The Complete Correspondence* ed. Joelle Biele.
- Arthur Rimbaud, *Illuminations* trans. John Ashbery.
- Tom Lubbock, *Great Works: 50 Paintings Explored*.
- Martin Gayford, *Man with a Blue Scarf: On Sitting for a Portrait by Lucian Freud*.
- Andrew Graham-Dixon, *Caravaggio: A Life Sacred and Profane*.

Peter Robinson

PETER
ROBINSON

PETER ROBINSON

On the Esplanade

'And with Thy Spirit' upon the water
this late afternoon there's a sunlit mist
blurring outlines on that Wirral shore:
there's nothing afloat but the marker buoys,
apparently no one in Cressington Park.
I'm trespassing, like, on its front once more
as into a general amnesia go
all the babies he baptised,
the thousands married, churched and buried,
who prided himself on his good funerals ...
'Remember them, dad?'
            'Do I have to?' he said,
those words come murmuring back to me
now low tide laps at mud and rocks
and I'm alone along the last
stretches of Grassendale Esplanade,
stopped by the wartime pillbox
still guarding an entrance to Garston Docks.
Then, look, two blackbirds, male and mate,
come pecking at somebody's dusk patio
as if life were a table laid.

Ein Feste Burg

'My hope to follow duly …'
John Ernest Bode

1

Towards the parents' trysting places
as coxes call out stroke-rates
again I'm entertaining fates,
mine among them, reading traces
to call on others' memories
from these rock-bulwark circumstances.

Gut-strung rackets in their presses
still, when I was young –
they're courting on a tennis court
one far post-war summer,
the pair of them, divided,
constrained between its lines.

Now as the Wear brings me round
back to where we started from,
its geometry of space is
filled with my attempts to reach them
and arriving, a survivor,
well, I shall restore amends …

2

I'll wonder then what were the chances
they'd be falling for each other
by this gorge's riverside,
(mum come down the road from Shields,
dad home out of Palestine)
falling along wood paths just taken
under ramparts, ivied walls,
that his regatta crew would throw
their winning cox into the water,
caught by mum's Box Brownie camera.
So I can see him now, see all that was to follow
duly hanging in mid-air ...

JEANETTE WINTERSON

© Peter Peitsch peitschphoto.com

INTERVIEW

TAKING A LIFETIME

Jane Davis in Conversation with Jeanette Winterson

Jeanette Winterson's memoir, *Why Be Happy When You Could Be Normal?* (Jonathan Cape, 2011) relates the story of her suicidal breakdown and subsequent search for the truth about her birth mother. It is also an account of a life shaped and given the deepest of meanings by books. As with Jeanette's favourite Shakespeare play, *The Winter's Tale*, the book falls into two halves separated by a wide and untold gap of time. The opening chapters detail the reality of the life that gave rise to Winterson's stunning first novel, *Oranges Are Not The Only Fruit*. Then, following a short intermission, the book flashes forward twenty-five years to 2007, when Jeanette accidentally uncovers her own adoption papers, and begins the painful and testing process of discovering her origins.

Jane Davis met Jeanette in Manchester for a conversation about the book in October 2011. What follows is an edited transcription interspersed with extracts from the book.

*

JW: The trouble is everything takes a lifetime, which I think is the best argument for something of us continuing after death. Surely you can't just work a thing out and then stop it? Nature doesn't *do* waste, does she?

My time was up. That was the strongest feeling I had. The person who had left home at sixteen and blasted through all the walls in her way, and been fearless, and not looked back, and who was well known as a writer, controversially so (she's brilliant, she's rubbish), and who had made money, made her way, been a good friend, a volatile and difficult lover, who had had a couple of minor breakdowns and a psychotic period, but had always been able to pull it back, to get on and go forward; that Jeanette Winterson person was done.

In February 2008 I tried to end my life. My cat was in the garage with me. I did not know that when I sealed the doors and turned on the engine. My cat was scratching my face, scratching my face, scratching my face.

(*Why Be Happy When You Could Be Normal?*, p168)

JD: *Tell me about your cat.*

Spikey. He's more like a dog. I've got two cats, Spikey and Silver, and they're my personality chopped in half. One of them is really outgoing, loves me and loves visitors, and the other goes 'Oh my God, not another person, please!' That's totally me in the cats. It was incredible that the cat was in there because without him I wouldn't be talking to you. The attempt would have worked, no question. He hates me going away. He sleeps on the bed and sits in my study and works with me. He looks out for me. You know in the fairy stories there's always an animal helper – that's what I got. Just at the minute when there was nothing else, and your brain can't save you, and your friends can't save you, and certainly you can't save yourself, there's the animal helper.

You've written a profoundly religious book. [JW looks aghast] *In the sense that the whole story is a story of love.*

I am sure that love is the highest value, I do believe that: it is the only thing you can set against the devouring principle, which rules so much else in our lives. We have to eat to live and that becomes its most grotesque with consumerism and the raiding of the planet that we do. We've never got a balance with our devouring instincts and I think the only thing that we do set against it is love acting as a check to say 'No, I won't take this, I won't eat this, I won't have this. I will *give* to this instead'.

I have the feeling that the garage was a kind of rebirth or transformation. You use the word 'done' – 'My time was up... that Jeanette Winterson person was done'.

Yes. It's odd those things stacked in the word. Done in, done over, done for.

I also thought it meant 'completed' – something is fixed. Ok, your friends and relations might laugh and say 'Nah, still the same old same old' but...

Oh yes, it is fixed and people who have known me for a very long time do say 'Yes, something enormous did shift'. Of course, the same old stuff goes on, but I know I'll never end up in the garage again. It's completely clear in my mind – I will die of natural causes or from something out there in the crazy world, but it won't be anything to do with me. That is 'done'. This now feels like a whole new chance and another set of things to get on with. I don't know where it'll take me but things have changed for me. I feel much more open, both forgiving of others and forgiving of myself, of how I used to be. There are points in your life where you can see 'I needed that then'. I would never have escaped Accrington if I hadn't been full of a sort of Protean energy and I was ruthless. I thought 'I'm *not* staying; you're not crushing me. I'm going'. I had to have enormous energy and self-belief to do that. But what's interesting is that then life will still offer you another challenge, that you're *not* done. That was a big shock.

I love the way you leave out those twenty-five years. Good! That's fine. Who the hell could bear to go through all that again?

I didn't want the book to be that kind of story. What interests me is that in our lives things don't lie side-by-side chronologically. They lie side-by-side in terms of their emotional effect, their weight, and what they mean to us. It's not to do with the calendar in any straightforward way. I wanted to show that in the book. It's a memoir but its also a story and this story is, amongst other things, about the overwhelming absence of one mother and the overwhelming presence of another. It has a certain linear trajectory but in fact life doesn't finally work that way – it's not linear and so the bit in the middle – those twenty five years aren't relevant to this story. So I thought, why can't I leave it out? I think that was right because what we want to know is where we go from there. The missing part is really the outworking of where I got to. I got there and I won some grace and I won some time, and went off and I did something with my life.

And then it all ends up in a garage.

It all ends up in the garage! And with no choice because – you don't choose it. You think from time to time, I could do this, and I think that is quite *freeing*. I don't think suicide or contemplating suicide is necessarily negative. Depending on the kind of person you are, you need to know that it's an option. I did. And that was useful for a while because I think the thought stopped it from happening but then there's a point when you're not thinking any more, and the psychic pain and the emotional pain is so overwhelming that – well, you're not thinking, you're simply trying to exit. It isn't rational. And no matter how smart you are, no matter how cared for you are – you know, I wasn't somebody with no friends – there's a moment where you cannot do it any more. I had to arrive there but by some good grace I was able to get through it.

There are so many fairy stories – you know them – where the hero in a hopeless situation makes a deal with a sinister creature and obtains what is needed – and it is needed – to go on with the journey. Later, when the princess is won, the dragon defeated, the treasure stored, the castle decorated, out comes the sinister creature and makes off with the new baby, or turns it into a cat, or – like the thirteenth fairy nobody invited to

the party – offers a poisonous gift that kills happiness.

This misshapen creature with its supernatural strength needs to be invited home – but on the right terms.

Remember the princess who kisses the frog – and yippee, there's a prince? Well, it is necessary to embrace the slimy loathsome thing usually found in the well or in the pond, eating slugs. But making the ugly hurt part human again is not an exercise for the well-meaning social worker in us.

This is the most dangerous work you can do. It is like bomb disposal but you're the bomb. That's the problem – the awful thing is you. It may be split off and living malevolently at the bottom of the garden, but it is sharing your blood and eating your food. Mess this up, and you will go down with the creature.

And – just to say – the creature loves a suicide. Death is part of the remit.

I am talking like this because what became clear to me in my madness was that I had to start talking – to the creature.

(*Why Be Happy When You Could Be Normal?*, p172)

Could you tell me about 'the creature'?

Oh yes, me and my creature. I was wandering about and we were shouting at each other. It was good to split the creature off. In technical terms I was crazy because I was talking to a split-off manifestation of myself that seemed real. As far as I was concerned, it *was* real, so it was a psychotic episode. But I think R. D. Laing's right about that – you sometimes have to have psychotic episodes and not drug them into oblivion, and not be so scared that you can't go through them. It is a huge risk but you have to take the risk because if you do medicate it or you fail it in any way it's almost certain that it will kill you in the end.

A lot of people give up at that point. They don't want to talk to the creature. They want to say, there is no creature. That kills you.

It does. Either you become a Stepford wife or it'll kill you. That's the alternative. And I think our world gets in the way of people going through the process. There's no space for it, and everyone's terrified of it, and that's why they thrust the pills at it. That's why I didn't go to the doctor. I felt I've got no chance if I walk in that surgery; it's going to be on my records. I was certainly lucid enough to work that out.

She was feral.
So I went to therapy and she didn't. Pointless.

It wasn't all pointless though, because after therapy, in Oxford, I was always so fed up that I went down to Blackwell's bookshop, and down to the Norrington Room, looking at the psychoanalysis shelves. The Norrington Room is a serious place – designed for the university, and stocking every text on brain/mind/psyche/self.

I had been reading Jung since 1995 – I bought the whole hardback set. I already had the whole hardback set of Freud, and I had always read Mind Body Spirit stuff, because if you are raised on the Bible, you don't just walk away, whatever anybody says.

Now, I was looking for something, and I found Neville Symington, a priest turned shrink, who had a simple direct style and was not afraid of talking about the spirit and the soul – not as religious experiences but as human experiences – that we are more than body and mind – and I think we are.

Symington helped, because I was getting well enough to want a framework in which to think about what was happening to me. Previously I had been holding on to the side of the open boat that was my life, and hoping not to drown under the next wave.

Occasionally the creature appeared when I was reading, to mock me, to hurt me, but now I could ask her to leave until our meeting the following day and, miraculously, she did.

It was summer. *The Battle of The Sun* [a children's novel JW had begun during the breakdown period] **was nearly finished. I was lonely and alone, but I was calm and I was saner than I have ever been, insomuch as I knew there was a part of me that was in madness.**

Symington talks about how the mad part will try to wreck the mind. That had been my experience. Now I could contain it.

A few months later we were having our afternoon walk when I said something about how nobody had cuddled us when we were little. I said 'us' not 'you'. She held my hand. She had never done that before; mainly she walked behind shooting her sentences.

We both sat down and cried.

I said, 'We will learn how to love.'

(*Why Be Happy When You Could Be Normal?* p177)

[Following this breakthrough, and supported by the loving relationship she created with Susie Orbach, Jeanette began the long-avoided search for her birth mother.]

I cried from about page 170 onwards and I cried most at the point where you are finding out what your original birth certificate says, finding out who you are... You say 'Susie held me'. Would any of this have happened without your partner, Susie?

No, I would have lost heart, I wouldn't have been able to nerve myself up to it because there are so many hurdles. At some point I would have thought, I can't do this.

You write 'She's smiling at me as the meeting begins and saying nothing, holding me in her mind. I could feel that very clearly'. So that's where I began to cry, because I suppose all of this last bit is connected to you finally being a baby and letting that baby be loved. I'm interested in the fact that the story comes here now in this format – memoir – because I think you've written it in it lots of ways, or parts of it, in your novels.

Yes, I have.

You've always been writing it. But here it seems really different and it feels like a breakthrough because it's able to use very straightforward, ordinary language 'holding me'. It's simple. Anybody could read this. That felt to me like a religious / spiritual / psychological / intellectual or artistic breakthrough that was to do with being able to give and receive that love, being able to be held.

I think that's probably true. I've always used the first person, which is unusual for a writer older than 25 years. I don't like the third person very much, although oddly I do use it in my children's books. What that's about I don't know – there's some shift there. But I think, this has taken a long time to move towards. I guess it was partly to do with my god-children with whom I'm very close and partly to do with everything that was leading up to this moment of seeing the birth certificate. That's the thing. It takes forever to get somewhere and then it happens with an inevitability, as though you were always going to get there. I think, insomuch as I'm alive, this is where I was going to get. Either I was going to die because I couldn't go any further or, having survived, I was going to be able to do this.

The moment where you are given the piece of paper with the names on it and you describe them as like runes… It's hard to read, so painful. It's the name of your birth mother and this is your original name: 'I am standing up. I can't breathe. Is this it then? They're both smiling at me as I take the paper over to the window'. At that point, that's where I was in floods of tears. It felt like a birth. It felt like being present at a birth.

I suppose that's true.

This creature who can't breathe and is …

It's true. I suppose they were both the midwives.

[In this extract, Jeanette speaks with Ria, the social worker who is giving her her birth information.]

Ria: 'I have counselled so many mothers over the years who are giving up their babies for adoption, and I tell you, Jeanette, they never want to do it. You were wanted – do you understand that?'

No. I have never felt wanted. I am the wrong crib.

'Do you understand that Jeanette?'

No. And all my life I have repeated patterns of rejection. My success with my books felt like gatecrashing. When critics and the press turned on me, I roared back in rage, and no, I didn't believe the things they said about me or my work, because my writing has always stayed clear and luminous to me, uncontaminated, but I did know that I wasn't wanted.

And I have loved most extravagantly where my love could not be returned in any sane and steady way – the triangles of marriages and complex affiliations. I have failed to love well where I might have done, and I have stayed in relationships too long because I did not want to be a quitter who did not know how to love.

But I did not know how to love. If I could have faced that simple fact about myself, and the likelihood that someone with my story (my stories, both real and invented) would have big problems with love, then, then, what?

Listen we are human beings. Listen, we are inclined to love. Love is there, but we need to be taught how. We want to stand upright, we want to walk, but someone needs to hold our hand and balance us a bit, and guide us a bit, and scoop us up when we fall.

Listen, we fall. Love is there but we have to learn it – and its shapes and possibilities. I taught myself to stand on my own two feet, but I could not teach myself how to love.

We have a capacity for language. We have a capacity for love. We need other people to release those capacities.

In my work I found a way to talk about love – and that was real. I had not found a way to love. That was changing.

I am sitting in the room with Susie. She loves me. I want to accept it. I want to love well. I am thinking about the last two years and how I am trying my best to dissolve the calcifications around my heart.

Ria smiles and her voice comes from a long way off. All of this seems too present, because it is so uncomfortable, and too far away, because I can't focus. Ria smiles.

'You were wanted Jeanette.'

On the train home Susie and I open half a bottle of Jim Beam bourbon. 'Affect regulation,' she says, and, as always with Susie, 'How are you feeling?'

In the economy of the body, the limbic highway takes precedence over the neural pathways. We were designed and built to feel, and there is no thought, no state of mind, that is not also a feeling state.

Nobody can feel too much, though many of us work very hard at feeling too little.

Feeling is frightening.

Well, I find it so.

The train was quiet in the exhausted way of late-home commuters. Susie was sitting opposite me, reading, her feet wrapped around mine under the table. I keep running a Thomas Hardy poem through my head

> Never to bid good-bye
> Or lip me the softest call,
> Or utter a wish for a word, while I
> Saw morning harden upon the wall,
> Unmoved, unknowing
> That your great going
> Had place that moment, and altered all.

It was a poem I had learned after Deborah left me, but the 'great going' had already happened at six weeks old.

The poem finds the word that finds the feeling.
(*Why Be Happy When You Could Be Normal?*, 185–188)

There's a terrible bit at the end of the book where you say 'The baby knows' – about the loss of mother, everything, the adoption.

Yes, I think the baby *knows*. You know that something has gone very wrong. I wonder, and I don't know about this, but I wonder if that absolute change for the baby prompts language early because that bit of your brain has to develop. You're desperate to understand what's going on around you. What am I going to do? I was talking about it to A. M. Homes in New York last week – I love her work. She wrote a memoir about her own situation called *The Mistress's Daughter*. Her father had a baby with another woman and that was her, and she was adopted. She thinks that when you do your search later it activates all this stuff which is in fact DNA material. She thinks it releases a chemical change because you've had to store this feeling or information. I asked her was she very precocious with language? And she said yes she was. You're seeking some explanation for why you suddenly land up in this place with all the wrong smells and the wrong person, so it may be so. We're evolved to survive aren't we?

What you've just said has made me think about dying and what you said at the beginning about 'Why have all this and waste it?' Being born and dying are the big acts of change. I don't think I know anyone who has died well.

Well, I'm going to. There's a great bit in Virginia Woolf, I think it might be in *Between the Acts*. Never having thought about death or dying before, the character suddenly sees it like a shark's fin out at sea, far, far away, and thinks 'What's that?' and then, of course, the fin is coming closer and closer in to shore. It's a nice way to describe the moment because you don't think about dying and then suddenly you do think, 'What's that?' and you realise it's mortality, and then you realise that it's my mortality.

And it's getting closer. When I first met my husband, he was about 28, 29, and he was obsessed with death and he has been all his life. And I have for many years been teasing him and just saying, 'For God's sake, we're alive, stop talking about death.'

And now he's come into his own! It's like wearing flares. If you just stuck with them from 1970 onwards, eventually...

They come back. So I just wonder whether that thing about before we're born whether we have some kind of consciousness of where we are even though we're not here yet.

I think we do.

Wordsworth says our birth is a sleep and a forgetting. If our death is something like that, I feel very glad for you that you have had your thing in the garage and now this time afterwards. There's a real chance now for what happens in the second half to be freer, more creative.

Well, I think it's going to defy the odds, actually. The cliché, and art's meant to be a cliché, is that then there will be a steady decline. Don't you think that Ted Hughes' *Birthday Letters* reinvented him? And then he died. It may be different for women because as we get older we tend not to turn into little tin gods, even if we've had some success, but men do and then they become ridiculous. They get all the praise, all the prizes, all the money, they don't ever have to do anything ever again really. And so they don't. It's easier for men to become rigid. But for women because nothing is ever safe, or ever secure, or ever certain, because gender politics are still at play, it may be that for that reason and also because women, like it or not, are in charge of birth, and therefore rebirth, we may be better equipped for the second half of life and all that it means.

The main thing I want to say is, you've been fantastically brave. It's a very brave book.

Well, thank you.

GILL GREGORY

Winter Sleep

Snowfall in Venetian blue
figures in a mist
and suddenly a child I knew
catching her death.

Words issued from my mouth
a baby in rough sentences
inhabiting breath

(I cradled and clothed her
in green silk pashminas)

the girl was quickly spoken
vocabularies stashing
our mouths to the brim

and before my very eyes she grew slim
as tall women threading their way

there were birds in the air
and light on our feet
that day we swept through

in turquoise swathes.

ESSAY

WAXING LYRICAL

Malcolm Bennett

I recently met a man (a bee-keeper *manqué*) who claimed never to have tasted his own ear wax. When challenged, he immediately played the religion card, claiming that he is banned from eating 'the wax of thine ear'. Citing scripture is truly the first refuge of the scoundrel. Of course, his assertion is not true, and demonstrably so as online interrogation of both the Talmud and Bible using the search terms 'ear' and 'wax', rapidly confirmed. However, it does beg the question, having hoiked a gobbet out with his little finger, if he doesn't eat it, what does he do with it?

Probably keeps it with his toe-nail clippings, would be my guess.

Further investigation demonstrated that while the ingestion of ear wax in private may go on, speaking of it – and possibly writing of it – seems to be regarded with some horror, at least among my (now mainly ex-) friends. With so many things nowadays the subject of relaxed discussion among social commentators and dinner party guests (this last is pure imagination – I can't remember the last time I was invited to a dinner party), why is a line drawn in polite society against something as harmless – indeed as useful and interesting – as ear wax? Cerumen (its medical stage name) contains antibacterial substances that help

AT THE BENNETT
SUMMER PARTY:

THE READER'S EDITOR GETS OUT MORE

prevent infection, and collects dust and other nasties that might otherwise cause damage to our ears. Different people produce either moist, honey-coloured, or dry, grey wax, these characteristics being inherited through simple Mendelian genetics, just like the colours of pea flowers. Some diseases can alter the colour and consistency of your ear wax, as does age. The distinctive smell and taste come from its being produced by glands similar to those that produce the sweat of your arm pits. Is nibbling ears merely a way of sniffing pheromones – organic, DIY perfume (home in three days, Josephine, don't wash)?

How can anyone not be fascinated by the stuff? Of course, sharing earwax with others, especially your pets, may not be so good for you. In a heroic piece of scientific research, Dr Robert A. Lopez, a veterinary surgeon from New York, famously transferred a piece of feline ear wax into his own ear to see (or, rather, hear) if the ear mites of cats can infect human ears. They can. 'Immediately, I heard scratching sounds, then moving sounds, as the mites began to explore my ear canal,' he wrote. What's more, the mites crawled across his forehead during the night to infect his other ear as well. The good news is that you can develop immunity against such infestations: having recovered, Dr Lopez re-infected himself and showed that, second time around, the whole thing was much less severe.

Incidentally, this reminds me of a story told by a colleague some years ago. His small daughters habitually bit their toe nails, something he and his wife found rather distasteful (although that may have been no more than jealousy – when were you last able to get your foot non-metaphorically into your mouth?) Coming home late one evening, he found one daughter chewing thoughtfully on a large piece of toe nail. 'Spit it out,' he said. 'I've told you before not to bite your toe nails.'

'Not mine,' she replied. 'Found it.'

The plug of ear wax from a whale acts as a kind of diary of the whale's life. The wax builds up gradually in layers of different colours according to the season and environment, and these layers, like tree rings, can be used to estimate a whale's age. What's more, pollutants and other lipophilic chemicals become incorporated into the wax, enabling anyone interested to reconstruct the exposure of the whale over its lifetime, which can amount to over 100 years.

'Why has so fascinating a subject as ear wax not been celebrated more in literature?', I hear you cry. Odysseus blocked up the ears of his crew with wax – but that's different. Where ear wax proper is mentioned, it is often in a negative context. Jonathan Swift gives it a brief mention in *The Lady's Dressing Room*, when Strephon, sneaking around Lady Celia's room, finds more than he bargained for:

But oh! It turned poor Strephon's bowels,
When he beheld and smelt the towels,
Begummed, besmattered, and beslimed
With dirt, and sweat, and ear-wax grimed.

Raymond Carver wrote a short story about an alcoholic man with a wax-blocked ear. There is the deaf man in *Captain Correlli's Mandolin*, of course, but that was owing to a fossilised pea rather than ear wax – although I am sure that wax gathered around the pea and made a significant contribution to the problem. I've never read Leon Uris's *QB VII*, but wasn't there a little boy at the beginning of the TV series who was cured of deafness by having his ears syringed? And I think that in one of the Shrek films, the eponymous hero makes his own cerumenous candles.

But that, as far as I can tell, is it. Does ear wax not appear anywhere else in the arts? Has nobody cooled it and sculpted a head out of it? Not even one ear lobe? *In Praise of Cerumen* is surely a title looking for a sonnet?

With the help of Google, I found a reference to a 2004 *Horizon* programme about synaesthesia, in which some poor chap could taste ear wax every time he heard the word 'Derek.' Of course to know that's what Derek sound-tasted like, he must have eaten ear wax himself at some time. And that, at least, makes him more normal, and ready to admit it, than some I could mention.

POETRY

THE OLD POEM

Brian Nellist

'Ceremonies for Candlemas Eve'
Robert Herrick (1591–1674)

Down with the rosemary and bays,
Down with the mistletoe;
Instead of holly, now upraise
The greener box, for show.

The holly hitherto did sway:
Let box now domineer
Until the dancing Easter day,
Or Easter's eve appear.

Then youthful box, which now hath grace
Your houses to renew,
Grown old, surrender must his place
Unto the crisped yew.

When yew is out, then birch comes in,
And many flowers beside
Both of a fresh and fragrant kin,
To honour Whitsuntide.

Green rushes then, and sweetest bents,
With cooler oaken boughs,
Come in for comely ornaments,
To readorn the house.

Thus times do shift; each thing his turn does hold;
New things succeed, as former things grow old.

ON 'CEREMONIES FOR CANDLEMAS EVE'

Herrick was a country parson in a small village in Devon, Dean Prior, south of Buckfast Abbey on the edge of Dartmoor and he sometimes hankers after the liveliness of the London of his youth. In the main however in an array of short poems he celebrates the customs, the food and drink, the sports, the young women of the remote spot he now inhabits, 'I sing of brooks, blossoms, birds and bowers'. *Hesperides,* his simple collection of 1648, has no apparent organisation but the reader finds himself, as the title suggests, in an earthly paradise, sensual yet strangely innocent, without that intensity of rapture and repentance in contemporary Metaphysical verse but with delight and sadness translated into all the objects of the countryside. This poem opens with the decorations for Christmas before Prince Albert imported German customs, when native evergreens decked house and church, rosemary, laurel, mistletoe and holly. At its date it is also a political poem since Puritans like Prynne objected to the corruption of Gospel piety by this adoption of pagan survivals. Herrick unappalled by such accusations refers tenderly to the old belief that the sun danced on Easter morning, just as Hardy likes to remember ox and ass kneeling on Christmas Eve.

But there is more to the poem than antiquarianism. That defiant opening, 'Down with' involves, behind the aggression, regret for the loss of the old decorations, not at Twelfth Night (January 6th) but at Candlemas, the Feast of the Purification (February 2nd). The calendar became a battle of the plants, 'Let box now domineer'. Everything has its season and the green things age even faster than us; 'youthful box' in a month or so gives way to yew, 'crisped' like the locks of youth. Today we hear much about 'garden poems' but for Herrick rooms become gardens; mainly planted with wild things, including fragrant sedges, 'bents'. The poet who wrote 'Fair daffodils we weep to see you haste away so soon', measures mortality in flowers. 'New things succeed, as former things grow old' with the paradox also that old custom is what he seeks to preserve.

THE READING REVOLUTION

DIARIES OF THE READER ORGANISATION

Sophie Povey

For the past six months, I have been working as Assistant Development Manager for The Reader Organisation. This role is new to the charity and reflects our increasing need to diversify our income as we grow. Most of our income is currently generated through the public sector and charitable trusts, but over the next three years it is crucial that we begin to increase the levels of income that we get from corporate, donor and community sources.

So how do we do that? When I described my new role to the little girl that I read with one-to-one ('I'll be trying to get some money so that more people can do what we do'), Molly offered me her week's pocket money, promising 'And there's plenty more where that came from'. Politely declining her heart-warming offer, Molly's response illuminated the fact that many of our friends and fellow readers do want to support our work in whatever way they can, and so when preparing our fundraising plan for the next three years, it seemed important that we begin to develop our 'Community Fundraising'. By inspiring and supporting the staff, beneficiaries, friends and partners who would like to take part, community fundraising will allow us to raise money creatively; from sponsored runs and cake sales to 24 hour read-aloud marathons and 'Readers Got Talent'.

I've been looking at how to expand the reach of Get Into

Reading and training into the world of corporate business. We've just embarked on an innovative project with Tesco that is providing a very exciting look at how The Reader Organisation can work in a business setting. This month, we delivered three *A Little, Aloud* workshops for Tesco Community Champions across the country, giving them the skills and confidence to deliver one-to-one shared reading groups in their local care homes. The relaxed meaningful approach to shared reading was new to many Tesco staff, and their feedback has been outstanding. The Champions report that shared reading will strengthen the quality of their community engagement, but also say that taking part in the workshop is impacting on their wellbeing at work: 'I feel genuinely lucky to be a part of this; it's such a valuable skill that will bring huge benefits'. I'm confident that the shared reading model could be utilised to improve staff wellbeing and development in other large organisations, and plan to work closely with Casi Dylan (The Reading Organisation's Training Manager) to make this happen. Not missing out on a chance to fundraise, we also had a charity 'Bag Pack' in Tesco Litherland earlier this month, raising a hefty £264 in three hours whilst Reader Organisation staff promoted the reading group running in the café every Tuesday evening. I'm very excited to see where the next six months take us!

OUR READER RUNNERS RAISED
OVER £700 FOR OUR WORK WITH
LOOKED-AFTER CHILDREN

THE READING REVOLUTION

THE JOURNEY BACK TO MY BOOKS

Heather Jones

Last week I facilitated two Get into Reading sessions. D, an eighty-five year old stroke survivor attended the first. Although she is able to read, she has cognitive problems that make it difficult for her to comprehend and retain what she reads. She always takes a copy of the story and poem home with her as she likes to read them to her sister who is blind.

At the second group we read Brian Patten's poem, 'Inessential Things'. T, one of the members of this group, is blind. We read through the poem several times at T's request. She said she really liked it because it describes how things feel, not how they look. I hadn't considered this when I chose the poem but once again something was added to my understanding of the text as a result of being part of this group.

INESSENTIAL THINGS

What do cats remember of days?

They remember the ways in from the cold,
The warmest spot, the place of food.
They remember the places of pain, their enemies,
the irritation of birds, the warm fumes of the soil,
the usefulness of dust.

**They remember the creak of a bed, the sound
of their owner's footsteps,
the taste of fish, the loveliness of cream.
Cats remember what is essential of days.
Letting all other memories go as of no worth
they sleep sounder than we,
whose hearts break remembering so many
inessential things.**

These two experiences led me on a course of reflection about the journey I have been on since becoming a Get Into Reading facilitator. We have an increasing body of evidence that shows the improvement in peoples' physical, emotional and mental wellbeing as a result of their being a member of a Get Into Reading group. But what do we know about the effects on (for want of a better term) a facilitator? Do we need to know anything about this? I'd like to suggest that we do.

I help to run two Get Into Reading groups as a volunteer. StokeReads is Stoke-on-Trent Libraries' Get Into Reading project. Reading sessions take place in a range of settings across the city: these include day care centres, mental health drop-in sessions, a high school and public libraries. It seems likely that volunteers are going to be increasingly in demand if we want to expand the project. An understanding of how the experience might benefit a volunteer might help with their recruitment. What follows is unavoidably personal and subjective.

Let me turn the clock back to December 2003 when I suffered a stroke as a consequence of a previously undiagnosed medical condition. I lost function in my left arm and leg and was unable to see at all for the first few days. I certainly don't want to dwell on my experiences of hospital and the frustration caused by my physical limitations. Over the first few weeks I regained the use of my arm and hand, and my sight improved slowly, but I was still unable to read. Prior to this experience I cannot remember a time when I did not have at least one book 'on the go'. Being a reader was a big part of who I was.

From 7am to 11pm the hospital ward was dominated by the television. There was no escape from it. My salvation came in the form of audio books. I devoured as many as my visitors could bring and discovered the deep pleasure to be experienced from being read to. I continue to indulge in this pleasure and I'm currently enjoying listening to Timothy West reading *Barchester Towers*.

Slowly things improved. After a few months I became able to read large-print books with the aid of a magnifier and a line guide. Then I was able to read large print without a line-guide. Eventually I was able to read normal print as long as it was well-spaced. My reading speed was considerably slower than it had been before but that is not necessarily a bad thing.

Before the stroke I had worked for over twenty years as a public librarian. I was used to being surrounded by books. My home was filled with books. I was faced with the prospect of seeing all of these books around my home and knowing that I was unable to read them. This was unbearable so I began to give my books away. Although this was a painful process it felt like a positive step, in that I was acknowledging and accepting my situation. When I say, 'I began to give my books away', perhaps I should qualify this statement. I kept every volume of poetry, all of my 'classics', and many other books I simply could not bear to part with. Many bags of yellow-edged, faded paperback novels that I probably wouldn't have looked at again anyway went to the charity shop. Not really such a calamity then.

Late in 2009 a former colleague from the library service who is a close friend was talking to me about a plan to set up Get Into Reading groups in Stoke. These groups were to be facilitated by trained volunteers. 'Do you fancy it?' she asked. Perhaps I should have taken more time to consider what might be involved but the idea sparked my imagination and I immediately agreed to become a volunteer.

I have come to see the Reader Organisation's training course at Burton Manor in Cheshire in January 2010 as a turning point in my life. I had settled into thinking of myself as someone who needed to read large-print books and I regarded most newspapers, magazines and books with small print as being 'closed' to me. In the weeks leading up to the training course I suffered momentary crises of confidence. What was I thinking of? Would I be able to cope? I need not have worried. The training was totally engrossing and hugely enjoyable. The opportunity to be completely absorbed in the reading – talking about reading and meeting so many fascinating people – was wonderful. I even managed to make good use of my walking stick in my portrayal of one of *Macbeth*'s three witches in our final night Shakespeare show.

My reading habits have changed as a result of this training. I am now giving time to reading some of the classics that I missed earlier in life. I also no longer feel compelled to finish a book just because I've started it. If it isn't proving to be worth the effort of reading it, then I put it aside. Perhaps reading more slowly has made me more aware of the quality of the writing?

If we turn the clock forward again to the present, I am now restocking the bookcases I partially emptied five years ago. I now consider myself to be a 'fully rehabilitated reader'. I still have a portion of my left visual field missing and when I am tired the lines on a page begin to move about; but I feel very fortunate to have recovered as well as I have.

And so to the future. Within the next few weeks a new Get Into Reading group will have started on the Stroke Rehabilitation Ward at the University Hospital of North Staffordshire. This marks a big step forward for the StokeReads project as it will be the first group to take place within a primary health care setting. I am looking forward to facilitating this group as it will bring several strands of my life and experience together.

The opportunity to become a GIR group-facilitator has been life-changing for me. Not only am I doing work that I enjoy and I feel is valued but it has also helped me to find my way back to being able to read the books on my shelves... and all those other books that are still waiting for me to read them.

THE READING REVOLUTION

READING *DANIEL DERONDA*

Casi Dylan

It happened half way through the session, and almost half way through *Adam Bede* by George Eliot. Mary was reading aloud with confidence, a longstanding Get Into Reading member, and part of a steady group who had opted to invest the next nine months of their time together reading the novel. Only today, half-way through, she suddenly broke off and said: 'Is it just me, or is anyone else finding this really boring?'

This is one of the most common concerns of trainees on Read to Lead courses: 'What happens if they find a book boring? Should you carry on with something if the group is not enjoying it?' Kate McDonnell, the facilitator in the *Adam Bede* group told me: 'The toughest thing about that comment was that it was more than a personal opinion, it was an invitation for others to switch off, to classify as boredom the natural difficulty of adjusting to the book's pace. The novel, all of George Eliot's novels, are driven not so much by plot as by mood. Her books are long because they have depth. I knew that I'd have to fight for it. It went down to a vote in the end and we did keep with it, by one vote. Months later, when we finished the novel, Mary's voice was first in praise: "I'm so glad we stuck with that. This writing, it's a bit like a psychiatry, isn't it?"'

There's a dual sense of duty here: a duty to the group, naturally, but also a duty to the book. Hence Kate's sense of a 'fight' seemingly *against* the will of the group she was there to facilitate. Of the hundreds of people who attend Read to Lead courses, the majority are familiar with a sense of duty to the group; be it in occupational therapy, teaching, community health working, or raising a family. The sense of responsibility towards the book is rarer and not so automatic, and it is this above all that Read to Lead works to instil and develop – the rewarding and sometimes obstinate thought that there's something here worthy of our attention.

George Eliot's *Daniel Deronda* is a book that I would fight for. When recently I found myself for the first time standing in the glamour of a Greek Orthodox church, watching my little nephew, Ioan, christened in the echoes of ancient unfamiliar chants – I understood it better for having read *Daniel Deronda*. The story is built on a relationship between the two young central characters, Gwendolen and Daniel. Gwendolen is a brittle socialite, seemingly very sure of herself, who loses everything and who must from desolation build a better life. Daniel is an aristocrat who, from the uncertainty of his parentage, has developed such a 'subdued fervour of sympathy, an activity of imagination on behalf of others' that he is at risk of losing himself in lives other than his own, until he recovers himself in his lost Jewish heritage.

Unfamiliarity and disorientation may well be the feelings that you as a facilitator will need to acknowledge when you begin to read the novel. The reader is plunged straightaway into the 'well-brewed' atmosphere of a high-class casino where Gwendolen is playing roulette recklessly. The room is scanned by an as-yet-unknown Daniel Deronda; we take in with him the striking young girl at the roulette table, 'Was she beautiful or not beautiful?', and the 'fifty or sixty persons' assembled around the table. 'Here certainly was a striking admission of human equality' – comments the author, as over the first two-and-a-half pages of the novel we are introduced in quick succession to 'the white bejewelled fingers of an English countess'; 'a respectable London tradesman, blond and soft-handed, his sleek hair scrupulously parted behind and before'; 'a handsome Italian, calm, statuesque'; even a 'melancholy little boy' in fancy dress, the only member of the party who 'had his face turned towards the doorway.'

As is often the case in George Eliot's writing, ideas seem to be born from the specificities of a given scene, which, in structural terms offers the facilitator an ideal frame and pausing points for group discussion, as in this instance:

> **But while every single player differed markedly from every other, there was a certain uniform negativeness of expression which had the effect of a mask – as if they had all eaten of some root that for the time compelled the brains of each to the same narrow monotony of action.**

It's an arresting observation, the 'uniform negativeness of expression' that chimes uncomfortably with the earlier 'striking admission of human equality'. As a reader, your brain is probably bristling with ideas, and the temptation for the facilitator is to dive straight into them, to question the impulses, joys and vices of gambling, perhaps, or the equality of all of us in our sins. But the effect of this weighty one-sentence paragraph is essentially cumulative, the idea does not exist *separately* from the scene that has been laid in detailed context: your facilitation, like the writing, needs to build up from particularities to ideas.

As simple a question as: 'Do you have a *picture* of where we are in this scene?' would better serve the writing and give the group a better place to begin than a question about ideas. The appeal to the visual is a way of getting straight at the impressions that have made their mark before the writing is thoroughly understood, and it allows you to jump over any inhibitions to do with language or vocabulary. It also offers a chance go back into the text to pick out key details that may have struck the group: those 'chubby nudities' perhaps, the 'light rattle', the 'light chink', the 'small sweeping sound' of the gambling house at work, the 'serried crowds of human beings.'

From this starting point, the discussion will inevitably take on a life of its own. But a facilitator should steer towards the human content. It's still too soon to go for the ideas. Instead go for the group members' individual experiences: 'Do you recognise any of these people?' or 'Have you ever been in a place like this?' Members will interpret this sense of 'place' differently: Harry, for example, who attended my reading group in Salford for many years, may speak openly about his former addiction to gambling, and could inform George Eliot's writing with experiences of his own in relation to a brain compelled by 'the same narrow monotony of action'. Others may pick up on the exclusivity of the setting – 'I'd never get into a place like that'. The tone of your questioning is crucial; you need to present yourself as puzzled but stimulated by the writing ('Does anybody know what a 'bedizened child' is, by the way? Or a 'serried row'?'), inhabiting the process of forming thoughts alongside the group, whilst simultaneously guiding towards a prior intimation of what the writing holds.

You may not need to spend too long on discussion at such an early stage of the book; in *Daniel Deronda* everything is intended to connect with everything else, so that ideas are revisited time and again under different circumstances. Just as Gwendolen and Daniel's eyes meet over the roulette table, so Mirah and Daniel's eyes meet over the water of the Thames, some 180 pages – and 12 Get Into Reading sessions – further into the novel:

Her hands were hanging down clasped before her, and her eyes were fixed on the river with a look of immoveable, statue-like despair. This strong arrest of his attention made him cease singing: apparently his voice had entered into her inner world without her having taken any note of whence it came, for when it ceased she changed her attitude slightly, and, looking round with a frightened glance, met Deronda's face. It was but a couple of moments, but that seems a long while for two people to look straight at each other.

A few hours later Mirah attempts to drown herself. She is saved by Daniel, who, guided by the strong impression of that gaze, returns down the river towards her. Drenched, lost, Mirah tells Daniel a little of herself – that she is a Jewess, that she has lost her mother and brother, that through Daniel's intervention she is: 'commanded to live. I cannot see how I shall live.' The chapter closes with Daniel's thoughts, as he takes the girl to the sanctuary of a friend's home:

Deronda felt himself growing older this evening and entering on a new phase in finding a life to which his own

had come – perhaps as a rescue; but how to make sure that snatching from death was a rescue? The moment of finding a fellow-creature is often as full of mingled doubt and exultation as the moment of finding an idea.

Not an idea but a human being. This is a tough, moving, important chapter, which touches on the darkest moments of despair and loneliness. It demands deep awareness and a light touch from the facilitator: 'What do you think Mirah is feeling right now?' would be permission enough to share personal experiences – especially at this stage of the group's reading life together – whilst containing (earthing) the feeling within the narrative. Group members often speak openly about their experiences of depression, of attempts at suicide even, of that sense of which Mirah speaks: '*Dolore – miseria* – I think those words are alive.' Such moments of revelation can be enormously powerful for the group and the individuals within it, and proof that Get Into Reading can create that space for sincerity of shared feeling. But it is important, especially at a juncture like this at the end of a chapter, that you are able to make use of the differences in perspective that the text offers you, to move the discussion to another place if need be. Because as much as this chapter could focus on Mirah's near-death, it is more concerned with the means of her life. This 'moment of finding' Mirah is so crucial for Daniel because it chimes within his thoughts with the sense of 'finding a life'. The timescale at work here is that of lifetimes, not moments – otherwise there would be no need for Daniel to question his having rescued Mirah. So why not put it to the group: 'Why would Daniel question whether or not he has saved this girl? She is saved, surely, in that boat with him?' The challenge of this chapter is contained in that hinged statement of Mirah's: 'I am commanded to live. I cannot see how I shall live.'

The first is a command, the second frighteningly in her own hands and utterly unknown. But this is where duty to the book is so important. The book gives little glimpses of other ways in which it might be possible to live and lets us pay attention to matters can be too dark or difficult in life itself. It holds open the space for the 'fight', as Kate put it, for that which as yet we do not know. We owe the book attention because it may in some sense save us.

POETRY

GORDON SCAPENS

Travelling Home

The map attempts
to show my relevance
in the day's purpose.

Information leaps at me,
route, distance, contours,
home reaches out.

But a map can't convey
the meaning of a journey
or a place of peace.

The destination is clear
but no welcome marked,
reward for a traveller.

Locked in its beliefs,
nuances the map lacks
are inside my head.

Flirting with the road,
I'm following a script
as old as time.

YOUR REGULARS

ASK THE READER

Brian Nellist

Q I saw the film of *Jane Eyre* recently and thought it well-produced and acted, stunning to watch and moving yet producing a very different effect from the book and notably simplifying, for example, the character of St John Rivers. Why does this so often happen with especially cinema adaptations?

A I'm sure you're right though I haven't seen this version yet. The book demands so much mental and imaginative activity in the reader whereas we surrender to the immediacy of the visual or, at least, I do. Certainly the timing of the two experiences, the conditions of their coming into being couldn't surely be more different, from several days of silent attention and reflection to two hours or so with an audience and, presumably, background music. The transformation is immeasurably greater than the realisation of a dramatic text in the theatre. The novel is mediated by a single voice, the style of the writing, but in *Jane Eyre* the contrast between the subdued life and the passionate inner dialogue of the principal character cannot be reproduced in any other medium. But there is a deeper problem, I think. Certain books achieve a reputation, become lodged in our mind less because of what they are than what we make of them. Our minds and memories simplify what the author has written to produce a different satisfaction to what we need, or think we need. We transform fiction into myth. Myth possesses a kind of geometry changing the messy reality of the book into a pattern of symbolic relationships.

Some books lend themselves to such a process though others resist it. You can't transform, say, *Middlemarch* into myth but we can't attribute this to a difference of literary quality. *Robinson Crusoe* is a great novel yet it becomes the story of a European and a black man alone on an island in myth, a story of colonialism. Friday is a Native American, probably a cannibal who only arrives on the empty island when Crusoe has lived there for twenty years or so. *Gulliver's Travels* is schematised into a contrast between little people and big people and their attendant distortions of the human but the rational horses get forgotten and the floating island and the absurd science of the third voyage simply disappear. The strangest piece of myth-making is probably the retrospective account of *Wuthering Heights*. The free passion of Catherine and Heathcliff on the open moors rebels against the enclosed and conventional marriage with Edgar Linton. Yet in the novel the last time that the 'lovers' are together on the moor they are twelve years old staring into the windows of Thrushcross Grange in envy of its comforts. Almost half of this 'love story' is devoted to the relentless revenge of Heathcliff after Catherine dies. The whole book is told by the visitor Lockwood from the account of the family offered by Nelly Dean and it is set not in the early-nineteenth century with all those glamorous clothes in the Laurence Olivier version but in a rustic late-eighteenth century with, presumably, knee breeches and frock coats. What we want though is something simpler and more elemental than the dry voice of Nelly Dean explaining that the Linton marriage would probably have worked 'but we must be for ourselves in the long run: the mild and generous are only more justly selfish than the domineering'. Films are made from the myth not the novel.

To return to *Jane Eyre*, we make of it what we want to be there in terms of our collective and contemporary concerns. In the novel, Bertha Rochester in her attic is the victim of hereditary madness as her brother knows and far from being an enslaved wife has been protected from the notorious private asylums of the day. St John Rivers is not a repressive Puritan, first cousin to Mr Brocklehurst, in contrast with the glowing passion of Mr Rochester. He is a Christian living the life of self-sacrifice who believes, which is indeed a possibility in the book, that Jane herself could endure such demands. When Jane escapes from becoming Rochester's mistress religious belief shares in the instinct to self-respect that drives her from the man she loves. The final words of the novel are not 'Reader, I married him' but reflections on St John's letter from the mission-field announcing his imminent death; it 'drew from my eyes human tears and yet filled my heart with Divine joy'. Film can't afford any more than our retrospective memories, to take account of that complex balancing of different kinds of value with which we might recognise a great good that is, even so, not a good for ourselves. Rochester himself repents of his offence against holy matrimony as well as against Jane in offering her a false marriage and offers atonement by trying to rescue the real wife from the blazing house. His maiming is not a feminist revenge upon the imperious male but the outward sign of his contrition.

I used to be excited by the mythic reading of literature in the criticism of Northrop Frye and it remains a valid element in our response to the book we read but it is less than the whole book. The truth, the *whole* truth and nothing but the truth' is what reading is about, where the truth means the words the author has written and our dialogue with the voice we hear when we read them. Disagree with them if you must but listen carefully first. After all the author has often spent as many years in the writing as we spend days on the reading and it is not unlikely that our hasty objections also occurred to them and there may be good reasons why the book is as it is. Don't alter it into the myth you want it to be, unless you are making a film of it, that is.

YOUR REGULARS

LONDON EYE

REVIEWING THE SITUATION...

This month marks five years since I started working in publishing in London. During that time, the number of books published every year has swollen by around 20%, and yet three bookselling chains (Borders, Woolworths and British Bookshops) have collapsed and another (Waterstone's) is under new management. Harry Potter gave way to *Twilight* which gave way to Stieg Larsson; the popularity of misery memoirs waned, while the market for angel books and books about plucky pets grew – which of course spawned a sub-genre of 'angel pets' and provoked the ASDA book buying manager to publically muse: 'A book that combines mis-mem, angels and dogs is our perfect paperback'. Richard and Judy's TV Book Club lost its power over the bestseller lists but celebrity autobiographies still dominate the shelves pre-Christmas, and when certain celebrities have published all eight volumes of their life story, they have turned to fiction, children's fiction, cookery, though with decreasing success. Over the last five years Jamie Oliver has barely been absent from the non-fiction Top Ten bestsellers (you can also see him every time you go into a Sainsburys, turn on the TV, open a newspaper, or go out for supper). Newspaper review pages have been cut but book-bloggers command ever larger influence. Libraries all over the country have been closed or threatened with closure, but a lively, passionate and widespread public outcry took politicians seemingly by surprise. Advances for authors have apparently fallen by up to 80% – £10K is the new £50K, but while I've heard of a début literary author being offered £500 I've also heard of other debuts commanding £500,000 at auction. Undoubtedly, mid-list authors felt recession-related angst more acutely, but conversely, as short-run printing became easier, the backlist became king – just last week Macmillan Publishers and literary agency Curtis Brown announced their mutually-beneficial joint imprint which will bring back into circulation the out-of-print works which have long languished on Curtis Brown's roster. In five years the boundaries between author, agent, publisher and bookseller have irrevocably blurred – publishers sell books direct from their websites, agents have turned publishers (Andrew Wylie's short term foray into digital publishing provoked uproar, meanwhile fellow agent Ed Victor unobtrusively opened a similar shop); meanwhile authors can bypass the lot and reach their readers direct as self-publishing becomes increasingly easy and attractive.

Most of these changes have been brought about by the impact of 'digital'. 'Digital' means different things to different people, but in this case it's my blanket term for digital book publishing and digital bookselling. Amazon were already a huge figure in bookselling by the time I arrived in publishing, and had not only independents but high street booksellers running scared, but then at the end of last year, ebooks, which we'd been warned about for years, suddenly *arrived*. On Christmas Day people bought more ebooks than physical books on Amazon, and most of those were through their brand-new Kindles. Amazon recently announced that sales of ebooks on the Kindle had overtaken hardback sales in the UK, and paperback sales in the US. Over the next couple of years we'll witness a clash of the titans and see Amazon vie against Apple and Google to dominate the landscape of digital bookselling, but in 2009 Amazon took a sure step towards that dominion when its first publishing imprint was launched – AmazonEncore 'helps unearth exceptional books and emerging authors for more readers to enjoy'. Most existing publishers are wondering, who are they 'helping' exactly?

Digital publishing is terrifying for some – barely a month goes past without a headline about the End of the Book. We can only guess whether ebooks will endanger or even replace their physical counterparts, or whether what we read and our habits of reading will change. The way we read – the concentration needed, the sparks and connections made in our brains – could be affected. The release of something like Faber's app of *The Waste Land*, a glossy, audio-visual, technicolor experience which surrounds the poem, sends a tingle up the spine for various reasons. It could be a vision of the way we will read in the future, with easy touch-screen clickable access to any amount of information *about* the book or poem we are reading. I heartily hope not, and I suspect that even if someone preferred it, they could not argue that the app is a substitute for simply reading the poem, unadorned. I've heard several of the more forward-facing and serious members of the new breed of digital publishers and innovators point out that apps are not marketing tools or a new breed of merchandise that we can churn out in order to better sell books, any more than apps can be replacements for books. Apps are a new product, and one that publishers could be particularly well-placed to create. At a recent conference I attended, the overriding message seemed to be that the raw material we search out as part of our existing day jobs – narrative, ideas, creative talent – will still be the staple of the digital future.

My search for that raw material hasn't yielded as much as I'd like over the last five years. My boss once told me that publishers fall into only two packs – the ones who see merit in everything, and the ones who are much harder to please. I've only read a few books that I really admired, and an awful lot of rubbish, so perhaps I know my pack. But since publishing was born in a crisis, and has lurched from quandary to crossroads ever since, my five years seems paltry; I'm still hopeful of being surprised.

YOUR REGULARS

THE LAST CANDLE

Ian McMillan

A few years ago I made a radio programme called *Home For Christmas*; I began it by describing a recurring dream I had, and still have sometimes although the making of the programme seems to have exorcised it a little, or at least made it less toxic and scary. In the dream I'm a long way from home late on Christmas Eve and I'm running through dark streets to a small country station because I'm desperate to get home. I gasp and sweat as I toil up some steps clutching my ticket and as I get to the platform the last train North puffs out of the station in a cloud of steam. A railway worker approaches me. He's got enormous whiskers as though he's on his way to play Father Christmas somewhere. 'When's the next train?' I ask. 'There isn't one' he says, and his voice is deep and boomy and tolls like a huge bell. He disappears and in the next scene in the dream I'm sitting in a cold waiting room at the far end of the platform and I'm weeping. Outside the cracked and mucky window snow is falling. I haven't got home for Christmas, and that's the worst feeling of all.

I guess I don't have to look too far or too hard to find the genesis of the dream. My dad was in the Navy and so before I was born he spent many Christmases away from home; I was two when he left in 1958 and one of my earliest memories (which could, of course, be a false memory and just a tale I've been told many times because I'm not sure you can really recall anything from the age of two) is of me and my mother running, on a cold winter morning, down the station in Darfield which didn't survive long after Beeching. The station looks a lot like the one in my Christmas dream, but this time we catch the train and go down to see my Dad on the *Ark Royal* in Plymouth. He's either just left the Navy or he's just about to and I remember standing at the bottom of some stairs with him on the ship and there was a man sitting on a stool, his head lolling in sleep. I've got a sense of Christmas decorations hanging somewhere but I could be making that up, too. 'Leave him' my dad says, and his voice booms like the man in my dream 'he's been on-watch' and for years afterwards I thought that when you were on-watch you were always asleep and that somehow by being asleep you were in charge of Time, and that if I woke up the man who was on-watch then time would slip and shatter and we'd all be off-watch and Christmas would never come, ever.

So for me Christmas has always been about a fracturing of normal time, a glittery mix of on-watch and off-watch. Junior School would end with a flurry of cards from teachers and a visit from Mr. Rothin the caretaker dressed as Santa and a walk home with my Auntie in the gathering dark. I'd sit and watch pre-Christmas specials of TV programmes like Harry Worth and the lighting of the fourth candle on the Blue Peter advent calendar. Unusually, I'd be at home when Mr. Coward the milkman called for his money, and I'd watch the strange ritual of Mr. Coward sorting out the odd Scottish pound note for my mother to give to my dad 'to make him feel at home'. I'd be in the front room when Don and Winnie and Brian called and Brian would play his squeezebox and my dad would sing in a high tenor. I'd be at home when carol singers sang at the door and my mother gave them toffees because 'they'd only spend money'.

But the one thing I wouldn't do in those part-frantic, part-still few days before Christmas was read. Normally I read all the time but I'd asked for books and annuals for Christmas and wanted to save up my reading time. On Christmas day there would be a flurry of annuals and Biggles books; *Oor Wullie* and *The Broons*, *The Beano*, *The Beezer*, a fat *Biggles Omnibus* as big as a breeze-block. I'd sit and read and read until my head lolled like the *Ark Royal* bloke and I staggered up to bed to read some more. Relatives who didn't know what to get me but knew that I liked to read would get me book tokens, strange cardboard currency to be spend in a country called Reading, which is only a little bit like Reading in Berkshire.

As I got older and tried to suppress the lump in my throat when they lit the last Blue Peter advent candle I bought books for other people, too. My brother was a lay preacher in church and I bought him a book of 18th Century sermons; my mother was guided by my taste so I bought her books that I wanted to read, like *Watership Down* and its strange successor *Shardik*. I bought my dad *Jane's Fighting Ships*, a magnificent catalogue of all the ships in the world and we'd sit for hours on the settee reading about the Polish Navy and comparing tugboats across African states.

Maybe, in that terrible dream, a book would have eased those chilly and lonely days in that shelter on that station. *Jane's Fighting Ships*, maybe, or *Oor Wullie*. Just a couple of tugboats to see me through to the day after Boxing Day and the next train home...

POETRY

PETER NICHOLSON

From Verse To Worse

Tired of verse, verse tired of me.
Next time round I'm dropping poetry.
Don't like myself or what I've become.

So to escape (impossible), I read an autobio
Half-price up the road – what do I get? More mess,
Male mess always the same – drunkenness, vanity, skiting
And, not-too-subtly implied, the sex stuff isn't failing,
Though something's failed if he thinks
Autobiography's kink
Can fool another writer with this stuff.
The rubbing up against the 'great' is sus,
The carefully scripted vignettes don't convince.

Of course I don't convince myself – am I a fellow fraud?
I don't think I am, but maybe that's just spam.
When the spotlight shines no-one's divine.
Greatness sits at your back
With the monstrous beauty you lack –
Shakespeare, Goethe, Dickinson, Wagner, all

Like Everests; we play in sandpits, calm
In our credulity,
Bubble reputations blistered out
With false bravado, suddenly in drought.
Stillborn rodomontade!

Publishing of verse seems quite corrupt,
Brought to light by suspect auspices,
Then written up by friends of friends of friends.
A few poor poets spend their lives in thrall
To those they think must matter, putting out
Like clockwork scores of books spread so thinly
That even those they sucked up to get shirty,
While futile special pleading in the quad
Can't get beyond the use-by date that mocks
Certainties which end delisted stocks.
Some editors will play the usual games
And publish minor poets with major claims,
Terrorise like Stalin on their patch,
Then from unlovely gulags troops dispatch
To the vasty deep of their bare rabbit hutch.
We watch them hopping back and forth for years
And give them letters for their poetry wars.

But that's them. I'm down
About myself and what I've failed.
Who's who in me – the onion skins reveal
Another and another layer flayed,
But what's at heart – genuine or fake.
(By the way, I judge myself, not you.
Keep your own counsel. I don't need
Your tepid charity.)

Poetry attracts some damaged souls
Whose poverty of spirit will appal,
The fatted, feral phonies who have plundered
Resources better spent on schools not funded.
Braying donkey experts do not help

Dropping in the barnyard theory pelts,
Not knowing once in all their footnote years
That poets must escape from what is geared
By *Psycho* shower scene limelight turns ill-starred,
Fascist eyries littered with the echoes
Of frantic voices, proved at end quite hollow.

Turn off the iron lung before the patient claims
Another swag of unearned tax largesse!
The question is: would this stuff get written
Without the gravy train.
If not, best they never chose
The literary life for their commercial pose,
Posturing in lieu of getting down
Something worthy of the laurel crown.
In the end good work will get done
And lick its paws before the borer wood,
When honour comes from serving what is best
Inherited by language, splendoured guest,
Evolution's prime and golden sign.

I throw that book against the wall and sigh.
Verse is tired of me, and I am tired of it,
And reading those evasions hasn't helped.
Time to plunge to sleep and know the night,
Beautiful, unconscious, and quiet.

BOOKS ABOUT...
TRANSGRESSION

Angela Macmillan

To transgress is to overstep a limit or to offend by violating a law. Just who sets the laws and the limits, be it God, the law of the land, or human morality, is the subject matter of the four books below which also explore how to live *after* transgression. The books recommended here concern Christianity but this does not mean they are of no interest to someone without belief in God. All reference to a Christian God can be translated into some other form of good. If we are not prepared to imagine this, we miss out on literature that is necessary for our souls – a religious word that many have already translated without too much difficulty.

R. L. Stevenson, *Weir of Hermiston*
1896, ISBN: 978-0192834317; also on Kindle

Lord Hermiston is a formidable 'hanging judge' who takes pleasure in his work. His son, Archie, attends a murder trial and subsequent hanging and is appalled by its 'tragic meanness'. He cries out, 'I denounce this God-defying murder' and is banished by his furious father to a remote hill farm. The novel is a work of maturity that sadly was unfinished at the time of Stevenson's death. Much of it is written in Scottish dialect which, strangely enough, is not so off-putting as you might imagine as it forces the reader to slow down and adds to the book's power and atmosphere.

Mark Rutherford, *Michael Trevanion*
1890, out of print but the text can be found in Google Books

To what lengths would you go to save the soul of someone you love? Michael Trevanion, a Puritan, is prepared to sin and face the certainty of eternal damnation to save the soul of his son. The huge question is asked in a short novella in which Rutherford probes deep into the human heart and spirit. The reader may have to translate into a contemporary situation but it is not hard to do. Mark Rutherford is the pen name for William Hale White. His loss of faith meant he never went into the ministry for which he trained.

Mrs Gaskell, *Ruth*
1853, ISBN 978-0140434309; also on Kindle

The old story of a fifteen-year-old girl, seduced, made pregnant and abandoned by a so-called gentleman. She is saved from suicide by a dissenting minister and his sister, who take Ruth and her baby into their home. It is a wonderful and extraordinary book about social shame and personal responsibility. *The Cambridge Guide to English Literature* claims that 'it is a book of its time and is hard to read today' – a typical, contemporary knee-jerk attitude to anything that remotely smacks of religion or sentimentality and entirely overlooks the abiding human content of Mrs Gaskell's work.

Anne Tyler, *Saint Maybe*
1991, ISBN 978-0099914709

Ian Bedloe is seventeen when he spitefully tells his older brother that his wife is having an affair. There follows a series of tragic consequences for which Ian holds himself responsible. Almost unable to bear his life under the burden of his guilt, he stumbles upon The Church of the Second Chance, a community of oddballs and misfits with whom he finds a way to carry on. It is not the Church but the people in it who offer Ian a lifeline. Read it for Anne Tyler's insight into ordinary, domestic life, and her ability to show the humour and sadness, the rightness and the wrongness in any given situation. She is a terrific novelist and this is one of her best books.

Fyodor Dostoevsky *Crime and Punishment*
1866, ISBN 978-0099981909

Dostoevsky wrote of himself: 'I am a realist in a higher sense; that is, I depict all the depths of the human soul'. This is the ultimate tale of transgression; the story of Raskolnikov, the student who convinces himself that he has the right to take a life. Don't imagine this is a difficult work of classic literature for the academic elite only. It's true that it is not an easy read, not because the language is difficult but because it forces you to think hard. Terrifying and exhilarating, it is a book that speaks to everyone.

A LITTLE *MORE* ALOUD

CHARLOTTE BRONTË,
JANE EYRE

Chosen by Angela Macmillan

Jane Eyre, an orphan, lives in the unloving care of her conde-scending aunt. Unable to bear the cruelty of her cousin any longer, Jane has retaliated and for such transgression has spent a terrifying night locked in the room in which her uncle recently died. Her aunt has decided to send her away to school and Mr Brocklehurst, headmaster of Lowood Institution, has arrived to meet his new pupil. This is a memorable moment in the novel and reading it out loud, brings the confrontation vividly to life.

*

'Who could want me?' I asked inwardly, as with both hands I turned the stiff door-handle, which, for a second or two, resisted my efforts. ' What should I see besides Aunt Reed in the apartment? - a man or a woman?' The handle turned, the door unclosed, and passing through and curtseying low, I looked up at – a black pillar! – such, at least, appeared to me, at first sight, the straight, narrow, sable-clad shape standing erect on the rug: the grim face at the top was like a carved mask, placed above the shaft by way of capital.

Mrs. Reed occupied her usual seat by the fireside; she made a signal to me to approach; I did so, and she introduced me to the stony stranger with the words:

'This is the little girl respecting whom I applied to you.'

He, for it was a man, turned his head slowly towards where I stood, and having examined me with the two inquisitive-looking grey eyes which twinkled under a pair of bushy brows, said solemnly, and in a bass voice, ' Her size is small: what is her age?'

'Ten years.'

'So much?' was the doubtful answer; and he prolonged his scrutiny for some minutes. Presently he addressed me – 'Your name, little girl?'

'Jane Eyre, sir.'

In uttering these words I looked up: he seemed to me a tall gentleman; but then I was very little; his features were large, and they and all the lines of his frame were equally harsh and prim.

'Well, Jane Eyre, and are you a good child?'

Impossible to reply to this in the affirmative: my little world held a contrary opinion: I was silent. Mrs. Reed answered for me by an expressive shake of the head, adding soon, 'Perhaps the less said on that subject the better, Mr. Brocklehurst.'

'Sorry indeed to hear it! She and I must have some talk'; and bending from the perpendicular, he installed his person in the arm-chair opposite Mrs. Reed's. 'Come here,' he said.

I stepped across the rug; he placed me square and straight before him. What a face he had, now that it was almost on a level with mine! what a great nose! and what a mouth! and what large prominent teeth!

'No sight so sad as that of a naughty child,' he began, 'especially a naughty little girl. Do you know where the wicked go after death?'

'They go to hell,' was my ready and orthodox answer.

'And what is hell? Can you tell me that?'

'A pit full of fire.'

'And should you like to fall into that pit, and to be burning there for ever?'

'No, sir.'

'What must you do to avoid it?'

I deliberated a moment; my answer, when it did come, was objectionable: ' I must keep in good health, and not die.'

'How can you keep in good health? Children younger than you die daily. I buried a little child of five years old only a day or two since, – a good little child, whose soul is now in heaven. It is to be feared the same could not be said of you were you to be called hence.'

Not being in a condition to remove his doubt, I only cast my eyes down on the two large feet planted on the rug, and sighed, wishing myself far enough away.

'I hope that sigh is from the heart, and that you repent of ever having been the occasion of discomfort to your excellent benefactress.'

'Benefactress! benefactress!'said I inwardly: 'they all call Mrs. Reed my benefactress; if so, a benefactress is a disagreeable thing.'

'Do you say your prayers night and morning?' continued my interrogator.

'Yes, sir.'

'Do you read your Bible?'

'Sometimes.'

'With pleasure? Are you fond of it?'

'I like Revelations, and the book of Daniel, and Genesis and Samuel, and a little bit of Exodus, and some parts of Kings and Chronicles, and Job and Jonah.'

'And the Psalms? I hope you like them?'

'No, sir.'

'No? oh, shocking! I have a little boy, younger than you, who knows six Psalms by heart: and when you ask him which he would rather have, a gingerbread-nut to eat or a verse of a Psalm to learn, he says: 'Oh! the verse of a Psalm! angels sing Psalms;' says he, 'I wish to be a little angel here below;' he then gets two nuts in recompense for his infant piety.'

'Psalms are not interesting,' I remarked.

'That proves you have a wicked heart; and you must pray to God to change it: to give you a new and clean one: to take away your heart of stone and give you a heart of flesh.'

THE READER MAGAZINE
SUBSCRIPTION INFORMATION

Pay via annual **Direct Debit** and enjoy our lowest subscription price of just **£18 per year**. You can print off a form from our website, or call us on 0151 794 2830, or if you prefer, email us at this address (magazine@thereader.org.uk) and we will send you a form in the post.

Or you can pay by **Cheque or Paypal**:

UK 4 issues £24.00 (including post and packing)
Abroad 4 issues £36.00 (including post and packing)

Please make cheques payable to The Reader Organisation and post to: The Reader Organisation, FREEPOST RSSL-UHCB-EKKE, The Friary Centre, Bute Street, Liverpool, L5 3LA. Don't forget to include your name and address, and the issue number with which you would like your subscription to begin.

Overseas readers: the easiest way for you to take out a subscription is by using PayPal on our website: www.thereader.org.uk.

Please direct email enquiries to: subscriptions@thereader.org.uk

READERS CONNECT

ALICE MUNRO
TOO MUCH HAPPINESS

Nita is recently bereaved, depressed and dying of cancer. Faced by a dangerous house invader (a man who it emerges is in flight

after murdering his parents and disabled sister), she experiences an odd moment of comfort: 'Then for the first time since he entered the house she thought of her cancer. She thought of how it freed her, put her out of danger' ('Free Radicals'). It's a crazy thought, and yet reassuring. Munro is good at catching the bizarre clarities of internal dialogue. The liberating effect of the thought doesn't last. Later Nina understands that her coming death from cancer cannot protect her from the fear of dying instantly; finally her life is more important than cancer, bereavement or depression.

Don't be fooled by the title – the stories are not comfortable to read. There is in many of them a load of unacknowledged guilt and then you have the panic of a rational mind avoiding itself, creating the structures of life around the very thing that can't be faced. More than anything her stories show the courage that is necessary to ordinary life. In 'Face' a man is able to find consolation in the place of his 'Great Drama':

> **Something happened here. In your life there are a few places, or maybe only the one place, where something happened, and then there are all the other places.**

As with Nina, he finds a point of view that allows something sure to emerge at the site of horror. I've called it courage and it's to do with a relationship to the strangely mixed voluntary/involuntary nature of events in your memory.

Lynne Hatwell (dovegreyreader) is a Devon-based community nurse

Compact and complete worlds such as the one in 'Child's Play' resonate long after the final word. The ominous opening gambit lingers like a bass note throughout, stoking the worry; how dreadful can this possibly be? In the end the tragedy comes masked in understatement, trebling its impact and leaving me hungry for just one more story... and another... and

* * * *

Mette Steenberg is the founder/director of Laeseforeningen, (The Reading Society) in Denmark

The first story in the collection reads like a novel. I was shocked to learn that I had to leave Doree at the road side – in fact I'm still haunted by those other 'Dimensions' and their inhabitants! – but I read on to discover more brilliantly told, disturbing, epic tales in short form. Loved every one of them!

* * * *

Drummond Moir, once of Edinburgh, works for a London-based publisher

'Fiction' centres on a musician, Joyce, whose encounter with a short story stirs up humiliating memories from an earlier life. Munro writes about the 'random and of course unfair thrift in the emotional fabric of the universe' with incredible feeling and precision; the only word for the way I felt after reading it is one that crops up again and again in this unsettling story: uncomfortable.

* * * * *

STAR RATINGS

***** one of the best books I've read   ** worth reading
**** one of the best I've read this year   * not for me but worth trying
*** highly recommended   0 don't bother

LEARNING TO READ RIDDLEY

Anna Lawrence Pietroni

I n Russell Hoban's *Riddley Walker*, thousands of years in our future, the people of Inland are trying to drag themselves out of the mud. Theirs is a post-nuclear society hungry for a story to make sense of what's happened. They have no creation myth, only hellish narratives of destruction played out in the Eusa Story and an inherited, tentative dream-fragment of 'boats in the air and picters on the wind'. English as we know it has been worn down and reconfigured, but while Riddley's world may be stumbling through a new Dark Age, his language isn't primitive. Riddleyspeak is direct, economical and energetic; we roadit, we meatit, we Norfed, we Eastit; a command is a 'Do It'; leadership is 'follerme'. The vocabulary of survival is snappy and efficient, fitting with the brutality of Inland life where you'll get eviscerated by wild dogs if you stray from the crowd and 'Sharna pax and get the poal' is less of a nursery rhyme than a prediction.

Riddleyspeak is at once familiar and strange. We have to slow our reading right down if we are to give ourselves any chance of understanding it in full. Riddley is 'walking his riddels' on paper and we have to read at a similarly steady pace, stopping from time to time to pick up a stone on the road or taking a moment to catch our breath. At first we may need to read the words aloud to ourselves to get the sense of them. Hoban provides us with a glossary and explains, for example, that 'pirntowt' is 'printout'. But much of the figurative language in *Riddley Walker* (blip, datter, programmit) refers to pre-conflagration technology of which Inlanders have no direct knowledge, so finding out that 'pirntowt' is 'printout' is of limited use: Hoban doesn't spoon-feed us with a meaningful translation. For a start, 'pirntowt' is a verb rather than a noun. We have to work out for ourselves what 'pirntowt' means to Riddley and deduce that 'I pirntowt' might mean something like 'I concluded'. If we simply 'translate' the word, we end up with only partial understanding.

We're justified in *beginning* to read *Riddley Walker* this way, moving from word to word and trying to reconcile Riddley's language with our own. We have to learn Riddley's language one way or another, and starting with vocabulary, at the level of the word or phrase, is one way to 'acquire' the knowledge we need to find our way about. Hoban explains how some names came about: Belnot Phist is a twisted-up Nobel Physicist; Belnot's father, Istoan Phist is a worn-down reference to Einstein. We could work our whole way through the text like this, untwisting 'Reckman Bessup' (who gives Riddley 'comping station' after his father's death) into 'a man who reckons up numbers as best he can'. But this word-for-word method won't serve us well. The just-enough-to-get-by, phrase-book approach would keep us moving through the text with a thumb in the glossary, reducing meaning to a series of transactions (swapping words in and out), as if communication were about words alone, each carrying a fixed, single value. If we continue to read this way, we're in danger of treating Riddley's text in the manner of Abel Goodparley, the smooth-talking Pry Mincer of Inland who moves from 'form' to 'fents' playing out 'trufax from the Mincery' in a puppet show. When he shares the Legend of St Eustace with Riddley, he says with unwarranted confidence, 'I can as plain mos of it.' As Goodparley's way of reading shows, when you try to 'as plain' a text, you mainly get it wrong.

The Legend of St Eustace is startling and disorientating even before Goodparley starts his exposition. The Legend is written in standard English so, after full immersion in Riddleyspeak for over half of the book, we're suddenly plucked out of one current and plunged into another. What's clear and fluent to us as Riddley's readers is at best opaque to Riddley and Goodparley, but Goodparley approaches the text as if it were encrypted and esoteric ('seakert'). He decodes, breaking the text down into dislocated units and mistranslates at every opportunity. It's a brittle, fragmented way of reading. He takes 'hamlet' and reads 'little pigs'; he takes 'St' and reads 'sent'. He interprets 'the open sea' as 'an open see meaning a look see': his own vision isn't just blinkered, it's utterly distorted and he's reading to find evidence to confirm his way of seeing the world. He reads for allegory and for alchemy. He wants 'teckernogical progers' and he's trawling the text for clues about how to make the 1 Big 1. (The two boys in the Legend, for example, become Goodparley's 'catwl twis'). He's hunting for a list of 'gready mints' and his *is* a greedy, grasping way of (mis)reading: "What can I get from this text?" not "What might this text have to give?"

Russell Hoban describes how he tries in *Riddley Walker* to cram as many meanings into one word as he can (so Riddley is the 'loan of his name' at the beginning of the book – he's the only person bearing this name, but it's not fully his yet. He'll only come to own it as he starts to live out what it means). If we take our lead from Hoban, Riddley's spelling should slow us down. For instance, when Riddley's world begins to destabilise, 'It seamt like the worl begun to roal.' If we read the Goodparley way, pulling out a word and translating it, we replace 'seamt' with 'seemed'. But in doing so we empty it out, replacing 'seamt' with a smooth but hollow shell of a word that we can slide comfortably over. Our 'seem' is not Riddley's 'seam': he is not holding up an idea of the world with one hand and comparing it to a children's toy in the other. If a 'seam' is the stitching together of two pieces of fabric to create something new, Riddley's two thoughts are so closely stitched that they form a new single piece of thought and experience, with the join still there if you look closely enough. But that's not all: a 'seam' is also a scar; it's a wrinkle, or a vein of coal pressed between the folds of the land. It's evidence of woundedness and it's where we mine, where we find our fuel, our energy. It's all of these things, a comment on the very nature of metaphor, packed up into 'seam'.

Becoming fluent in Riddleyspeak means *not* smoothing out what might feel like bumps in the text. If we slip too quickly past the 'yes' in Riddley's 'onlyes', we miss the endorsement folded into 'the onlyes power is no power' and the not-so-much coded as screaming 'No' at the core of the 'clevver' search for knowledge, for the 'Nos of the rain bow' that ultimately leads to the devastating 1 Big 1. If we get too accustomed to reading 'No.' as 'number' we may not be mistranslating, but we create a text that's blunted and less nuanced.

Along with words folded into other words, there are little spaces in the text that speak, and it would be all too easy to miss them. It matters that Riddley writes 'be come' not 'become': he unhooks words from each other and gives them room to move about. We are used to hearing a word in a certain way because we know the shape of it and how the weight of it will settle, but when Riddley separates familiar words to make a new phrase, the weight shifts and we have to carry the phrase more consciously. The phrase means something different: the words within it have a different value and, together, a different resonance. When the central quest in *Riddley Walker* is to 'the hart of the wud its the hart of the wanting to be', there is a hospitality, a homecoming, in this new phrase 'be come'. The space matters and if we listen to it, we hear Riddley's longing all the more clearly.

Sometimes the space operates in a subtly different way: it doesn't so much transfigure meaning as show us how Riddley's world shapes his thinking. Take 'to gether': it's important that we 'read' and sustain the gap between the words. 'To gether' is related to our word, but it's not just an uncoupled version of 'together'. Riddley is a forager from How Fents so 'gethering' is a means of sustenance and of survival. In that 'to gether' there is a gathering of scattered parts, a harvesting. His 'to gether' is his way of life; it's not the same as my 'together.'

We must also resist the temptation to use synonyms as a short-cut to deeper understanding. 'To lose out of memberment', for example, is not 'to forget'. My objection is more than resistance to recasting the rhythm of a sentence; it's not about a nuanced difference of degree (say, between Hoban's double-cream and my skimmed milk): just as 'hamlet' does not mean 'little pig', when Riddley writes about 'losing out of memberment', he doesn't mean 'forgetting'. In the destruction (rather than creation) myth,

'Why the dog wont show its eyes', the man and woman 'los out of memberment the shapes of nite'. This isn't absent-minded-ness, it's a profound alienation from something primal in their own nature, from '1st knowing'. In Inland, the communities are either 'form' or 'fents' (only the dyers and charcoal berners live outside the bounds). They're farmers or they're foragers – either way they only travel armed and 'crowdsafe', then retreat into fortified compounds at night. To 'keap in memberment' is to more than to remember; it's to keep something within bounds and alive. To 'lose out of memberment' is to cast out into the wild night. If, like Goodparley, we look for equivalence, trading one word for another, ('that for you and what for me?'), we risk reading narrow (as distinct from reading close).

Even when we become fluent in Riddleyspeak, his own 'spel' sounds out the roll-call of his themes. Meaning is sustained as echo through a sequence of separate, repeated words sounding out across the narrative: I notice 'hoal' and 'poal', for instance, because they don't look like 'hole' or 'pole', and then because their rhyme calls out back and forth across the text. The hoal and the poal are never good places to be: Brooder Walker, Riddley's dad, dies in a 'hoal' crushed by a 'girt old black machine' when the winch slips. The Ardship of Cambry is imprisoned in a hoal ('Sharna pax and get the poal, when the Ardship of Cambry comes out of the hoal'). Hoals are where you wait before you die, and the poal (a tool of government) is waiting, ready for your head: 'These heads ben telling'. The hoal and poal echo in Riddley's craving to 'jus see 1 thing clear the **woal** of whats in it' and there is an ultimately liberating acceptance in Riddley's realisation that 'you cant stay hoalt up' as he steps out onto the road, 'in fear and tremmering only not running a way.' 'Riddley Walker' has become his 'oan' name': he's independent and he's not the 'loan' of it any more.

I thought at first to compare Riddleyspeak with the sacred, abused Eusa Folk, the descendents of the 'Puter Leat', responsible for the 1 Big 1 and subsequent Bad Time. The Eusa Folk look like they've been 'shapit qwick and rough out of clay' with 'faces like bad dreams' and 'every kynd of crookitness'. But this comparison would suggest that Riddleyspeak is somehow a mutant variant on a norm, a nightmarish 'crookitness' that needs to be put straight. Ultimately it's not Riddleyspeak which resembles the misshapen Eusa Folk, but Goodparley's own 'terpitations' which operate like genetic misreadings, like warped coding. Goodparley fears words. He acknowledges their power: "Words! Theywl move things you know theywl do things. Theywl fetch." If we read fearfully like Goodparley – fixing meaning and trading words like cuts of hash, eliding differences and sliding over (rather than acknowledging) the parts we don't understand, seeing the text as 'crookit' and trying to make it 'strait' – we're left with bad translation. It's a mannered reading that's controlled and pragmatic, depleting both text and reader. Riddley himself offers a different way. A 'Riddley' reading doesn't try to 'as plain'. He comes 'in emtyness and ready to be fult.' I think Iwl yes with that.

ANNA LAWRENCE PIETRONI

© Tom Weller

YOUR RECOMMENDATIONS

A FEW GOOD BOOKS

FOR TEENAGERS

Anna Fleming

Jack London, *The Call of the Wild*
ISBN 978-0192728012

Journey with Buck, a German Shepherd-Saint Bernard cross, into the wild, frozen north of Canada. It is a compelling and fascinating read. Alongside Buck you learn about a more primitive existence which is essential in such a harsh and extreme environment. As civilization is stripped away, Buck embraces his prehistoric, wild nature, and the reader also confronts humanity's origins. Part of the excitement of this novel is the dog violence, so be warned!

Philip Pullman, *Northern Lights*
ISBN 978-0439951784

Another fantastic adventure story into the Arctic Circle. I would recommend this as a book to share: read it with a group, or have others around who've read it. The story triggers so many deep thoughts, questions and ideas that discussion is essential. Chats about the children's Daemons (animal companions every human is attached to) have ranged from exploring loss and loneliness, to trying to describe a relationship closer than friendship and family. Everyone brings a unique understanding to the story, its fascinating!

Charles Dickens,
A Christmas Carol
ISBN 978-0099529736

The Christmas classic, remind yourself of the true meaning and significance of Christmas spirit. Scrooge's personal journey is engaging: from aversion to pity, the reader can't avoid feeling strongly. His opportunity of redemption is ultimately uplifting, and the Spirits provide an exciting supernatural dimension to this thought-provoking story.

FOR CHILDREN AGED 8–12 YEARS

Patrick Fisher

J. Heinrich Hoffmann, *Struwwelpeter*
ISBN 978-0486284699

These short cautionary verses were written by Hoffman for his sons as a Christmas present when his wife deemed the blank pad and pen he had bought as insufficient. Shocking, hilarious and at times scary these stories of misbehaving children meeting their makers are brilliant to read aloud and have excellent accompanying pictures.

ill Tomlinson, *The Penguin Who Wanted to Find Out*
ISBN 978-1405210850

An absolute must for all animal lovers. Otto is the first penguin chick to be born that year so he has to show all the other chicks how to swim, catch fish and toboggan but who will teach Otto if all the adult penguins seem preoccupied with other things?

This is a wonderfully warm story about discovery, adventure and growing up and the cast of brilliant Antarctic animals Otto meets on the way will have you smiling long after it's finished.

C.S. Lewis, The Lion, *the Witch and the Wardrobe*
ISBN 978-0006716778

If you know somebody who has yet to meet Mr Tumnus and Aslan then remedy that immediately with this book. Escaping through the back of a wardrobe to Narnia, where it is always winter, Lucy, Edmund, Peter and Susan become caught up in the terrifying rule of the White Witch. Their lives are soon in danger and even the trees cannot be trusted. Can talking beavers, Father Christmas and the mysterious Aslan, who is on the move, really help before it is too late?

Although second in a series of seven this book stands alone as a classic.

FOR CHILDREN UNDER 8 YEARS

Samantha Shipman

Michael Foreman, *Mia's Story*
ISBN 978-1844282784

This is my favourite book to read with children of this age, it never fails. Mia is a young girl living in the snowy mountains near Santiago in Chile. Mia's Papa works hard every day selling scrap in the city and dreams of one day being able to build a house of bricks for his family. When Mia loses her dog she goes on a journey to find him which leads her higher up into the mountains to a place in the stars where she gathers a clump of flowers that begin to transform her life and the lives of those around her.

Jill Barklem, *Brambly Hedge: Winter Story*
ISBN 978-0001837119

One of the much loved Brambly Hedge stories, I would highly recommend reading it this winter. The Brambly Hedge stories are timeless and magical, and this one particularly captures the imagination. Snow has come to Brambly Hedge and deep drifts cover the windows and doors, many of the children haven't seen the snow before and look out on it with great excitement. The mice decide to follow in the tradition of their forefathers and hold a Snow Ball, working together they create a sparkling ice hall and fill it with food, friends, and family.

Michael Foreman, *The Cat on the Hill*
ISBN 978-1842704714

This beautifully-illustrated book grabs children's attention from the first page and is impossible to put down. The Cat on the Hill is the story of a stray cat living in St Ives who until recently spent his life on the fishing boats every day with an old sailor. The story follows the cat through the seasons, giving the reader a picture of life in St Ives whilst showing how the cat learns to adapt to his new surroundings helped by the friends he makes along the way. The story focuses on the importance of friendship and ends with a traditional Christmas message. This is a moving and heartwarming story, perfect to read aloud on a cold and dark winters night.

BUCK'S QUIZ

WHAT'S IN A NAME?

Angela Macmillan

1. Which novel is subtitled 'The Radical'?
2. Where is Enoch Arden when his wife thinks him dead?
3. Who wakes to find 'an angel writing in a book of gold'?
4. A pair of gamblers place a bet concerning the transportation of a glass church. In which novel?
5. Which book takes the form of a wife's letters to her husband about the terrible killings her son has done?
6. Which maiden 'lived with no other thought/ Than to love and be loved by me'?
7. Mallards in Tilling and The Hurst in Riseholme are the resspective houses of which fictitious pair?
8. 'O is he dead then? my duty all ended, / Who have watched his mould of man, big-boned and hardy-handsome'? Who is this farrier?
9. A Jewish, 48 year-old anti-hero writes letters compulsively to the living and the dead. Who is he?
10. 'I could not love thee dear so much, / Loved I not honour more'. To whom is the poet singing?
11. Which controversial novel is subtitled 'The Confessions of a White Widower Male'?
12. Whose story begins on the ship, the *Patna*?
13. 'When we were first acquent;/ Your locks were like the raven'. Who is she addressing?
14. Who are the brother and sister whose names become the title of the third volume of a trilogy?
15. In which novel do we hear of 'that first secret drink of golden fire… never to be forgotten'?

THE READER CROSSWORD

Cassandra   No.36

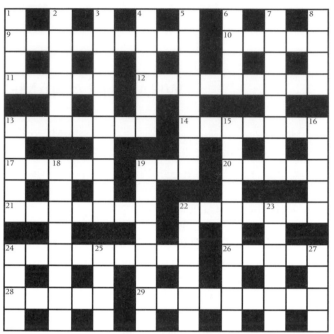

ACROSS

9. Combination of bun and pie for effective pain relief (9)

10. Starting our trip here each route is different (5)

*11, 4 & 15 down. Scottish peak of teaching talent (5, 2, 4, 4, 6)

12. Steam train on course for Derby perhaps? (4, 5)

13. Attacks Ratty's friend on streets (7)

14. Small space meets urges (7)

17. 16 down in Italy perhaps? (5)

* 19 & 24. Followers of Benedick form a group (3, 9)

20. Wherein Lord Sugar guesses the cause of dispute (5)

*21 & 13 down. 2 down's girls have few resources (7, 5)

22. Shaggy dog story cut short? (7)

*24. See 19 across

26. Neat trimming attached to the yoke (5)

*28. See 2 down

29. My boss is one disposed to close association (9)

DOWN

1. Effete little devil from the left (4)

*2 & 28 across. Author of UK arms peril fiasco (6 5)

3. Reductants dissolving into condiment carrie (5, 5)

*4. See 11 across

5. Once gone away potentially dangerous (8)

6. Shampoo highlights into rather dim animal (4)

7. Appealing but maybe like a witch (8)

8. Language expressed in bitter sentences (4)

*13. See 21 across

*15. See 11 across

16. Suspect rodent? (5)

18. Ulster varnish (8)

19. Circulating, I rest too often, not the speedies (8)

22. Brushes for northern women (6)

*23. 2's lady in charge at Crewe (6)

24. Not essential for good wine or a presiden (4)

25. In Minsk leopards cause deer to retreat (4)

27. Recommended direction for young man (4)

*Clues with an asterisk have a common theme

OXFORD
UNIVERSITY PRESS

PRIZES

The winner of the Crossword (plucked in time-honoured tradition from a hat) will receive a book prize courtesy of Vintage Classics, and the same to the winner of the fiendishly difficult Buck's Quiz.

Congratulations to Tony Anstey from Birkenhead (Buck's Quiz), and to Steve Bonkett from Cardiff (Crossword competition).

Please send your solutions (marked Cassandra Crossword or Buck's Quiz) to The Reader Organisation, The Friary Centre, Bute Street, Liverpool, L5 3LA.

ANSWERS

CASSANDRA CROSSWORD NO. 35

Across
7. Auction 8. Station 10. Circle 11. Narrator 12. Toga 13. Lifestyles 14. Counterplot 19. Dance to the 22. Time 23. Cavatina 24. Molly's 25. Anthony 26. Endgame

Down
1. Music of 2. Staccato 3. Powell 4. Starts up 5. At Lady 6. Coroner 9. Ineffectual 15. Nutrient 16. Ontology 17. Lasagne 18. Empyema 20. Cha cha 21. Ermine

BUCK'S QUIZ NO. 43

1. Richard II 2. The Talisman 3. 'Drake's Drum', Henry Newbolt 4. *Ragtime*, E.L.Doctorow 5. *I Claudius* 6. *The Eagle of the Ninth*, Rosemary Sutcliffe 7. Sir John Moore after Corunna 8. *The Madness of George III* 9. *The Balkan Trilogy*, Olivia Manning 10. 'Easter 1916', W.B. Yeats 11. *The Blue Flower*, Penelope Fitzgerald 12. Julius Caesar 13. *Romola*, George Eliot 14. Nancy Mitford 15. Hilary Mantel, *A Place of Greater Safety*

FICTION

SHINE

B. J. Epstein

Viktor lifts up a pair of dull black pumps, the narrow high heels worn down around the edges, holding them before his eyes, letting his vision blur against the faded dark material. He breathes in the vaguely sweaty leather combined with a hint of sweet perfume and the smell comforts him. Sighing, he brings the shoes briefly to his chest, hugging them to his body, before placing them carefully on a cushion of old Sunday newspapers.

They are Simone's shoes and Viktor can see where her crooked little toes have pushed against the leather, stretching it out into two tiny, misshapen hills on the outer sides of the pumps. He can see, too, how she rubbed her heels on the backs of the shoes, perhaps in the motion of a nervous habit, so that the material has folded over slightly. They are not new shoes; they are well-used, shabby, broken shoes, but Viktor thinks, for just a moment, that he has never seen shoes more beautiful.

B. J. EPSTEIN

He takes a piece of fine chamois and rubs it over the shoes, trying to remove all the dust and dirt. And then, slowly, Viktor starts to polish Simone's shoes, making the leather cleaner and more shiny than it has ever been, even on the day Simone bought them. He bends over the shoes, smoothing out their wrinkles and imperfections, making them glossy with wax, massaging them as tenderly as though they were her actual feet. There is a sore ache in his lower back, a pain that snakes around his body and pulses into his heart, and he hears the heavy hammering of the rain on his windows, but he continues shining.

* * *

It was mainly men who came to Viktor's stand in Union Station, men in pin-striped business suits, carrying the *Wall Street Journal* in one hand, a calfskin briefcase in the other. Viktor knew some guys, mostly other shiners and a few barbers, who rarely saw women in their shops or at their stands, and they took this at evidence that men cared more about their appearance, but Viktor didn't agree. 'Women have other things going for them,' some of Viktor's friends said, 'and they don't need to pay attention to the little details.' The men guffawed rawly, thinking about exactly what else women had going for them.

'Oh, I don't know about that,' Viktor usually said in his unhurried, thoughtful way. He thought about the way his mother had stayed home, quietly cooking and cleaning for him and his father, wearing the same faded dress and tired slippers, her hair unstyled. 'I think women just don't feel like they deserve such special treatment, so they don't come.' His friends laughed and said he didn't know much about women if he thought that and they told him about their demanding wives and girlfriends and soon they were trying to top one another with tales of needy, greedy women, and Viktor sat quietly, listening to their coarse sing-song.

One morning, a woman suddenly parted from the noisy crowd flowing from Track Seven and Viktor, who was crouching by the foot of the chair, ready for the hurried commuters who wanted a quick touch-up before work, realized with surprise that this woman was coming towards him. She looked straight ahead, walking confidently, and she didn't hesitate before climbing into the chair. Her voice was loud and haughty. 'Shine, please.'

Viktor nodded and got to work, concentrating on her scuffed navy pumps, not allowing himself to look at her pretty face, which he'd already noticed was slender and oval-shaped, with big brown eyes over a little, pointy nose. He polished, careful not to stain her pale pantyhose, and listened to her quiet, toneless humming. She jiggled her right leg when he worked on the left shoe, and then the left when he moved to the right. Viktor finished and she stood up, her chin high, grinning with pleasure. Her legs were thin, sticking out from her plain dark suit like twigs and the pumps seemed too big, too dangerous, for her.

The woman thrust a handful of bills at him and rushed away before he could thank her. When Viktor reached for his wallet and started to sort the money, he realized that this woman had given him a fifty percent tip. His prices were listed on a board beside the chair and he thought that she must have seen them. He squatted again.

Viktor thought he'd have to remember to tell his friends that he had had a lady customer and that she'd seemed as concerned about her appearance as any man. He quickly changed his mind, however, and decided that he wanted to keep this customer a secret, though he didn't know why.

* * *

A few mornings later, the woman was back, in a pair of gray heels that neatly matched her crisply tailored suit. It was barely eight in the morning, but she looked alert and energetic, and she tapped her pink-painted nails against the armrests impatiently. Her chipper voice echoed in the marble lobby of the station. 'Shine, please.' Again Viktor polished her shoes silently, trying not to let himself admire the woman's creamy skin or her glossy brown hair, pulled loosely into a braid, or her shapely hands. She left the stand as soon as he was through, pressing the payment and the too-high tip into his dry, polish-stained hands.

It was during her fourth shine that she first really spoke.

Viktor was pulling the rag over the shoes for the final time, getting rid of any last stubborn specks of dust, when she leaned over, putting her face just inches above his. She said, 'You know, I still can't believe I'm doing this.' She sounded younger now, less certain, and she giggled self-consciously.

Viktor sat back on his heels, but he didn't dare meet her gaze. He'd never been good with women; he'd been shining shoes since he was a boy and his father ran this stand, and Viktor had been so surrounded by men all his life that sometimes he was startled even by the sight of a woman. He'd dated a little, but only when the women had asked him, women he'd gone to school with or met through his friends, and they'd usually complained about his shyness and the trembling way he attempted to kiss, before leaving him. He didn't mind and he was accustomed to the idea that women would always be an unknown other for him, but he had to admit that there were times – not so often, but still frequent enough to sadden him – when it hurt to listen to the easy way his friends talked about their wives and about their comfortable, generally happy lives. He felt a pounding in his chest and he wondered what could happen with this woman. Finally, Viktor looked up timidly. 'What do you mean?'

She giggled again. 'I've always wanted to get my shoes shined like this. My father used to get his shoes shined every morning before work. Sometimes I went with him. He sat in that chair like a king, caring about nothing but how shiny his shoes would be.'

Viktor laughed, nervously. He'd never thought about what the men might be thinking while he shined their shoes and he'd never imagined what it would be like to be the customer. He hadn't sat in that chair himself, except for when he was a kid and got tired of squatting, and his father allowed him to rest in that chair for just a few moments during off-times, until snapping that he'd been sitting there being lazy long enough and that that chair was for paying customers, not idle children.

'Well,' the woman said when Viktor didn't respond, 'I guess I just always wondered. Now I know.' She wasn't smiling anymore. She stood up to go.

Viktor mumbled, 'So is it relaxing?' He immediately regretted asking that.

She tilted her head and her hair, which was loose around her shoulders, swung forward, releasing a soothing flowery scent. Usually he breathed in the strong fumes from shoe polish and mink oil, along with his customers' sweat and cologne and newsprint, and the delicate sweetness of this woman's hair surprised him. She said, 'It is, yes. Thank you.'

Viktor nodded, but wasn't sure what more he could say, so he started shifting his bottles of polish and wax around, organizing them by color and size, his hands with their greasy brownish nails moving smoothly among the containers. He heart beat too quickly.

After a pause, she said, 'I'm Simone.' She held out her hand to him.

Viktor, still crouching on the ground, looked up again. A few strands of hair cut across Simone's cheeks and they looked almost like scratches. He thought that he would like to take some white polish and rub it gently over her face, making those flaws disappear into a clean evenness, but he immediately dismissed this desire as foolish, and then he stretched out his hand to hers. Her skin was soft, even buttery, and a velvety tingle caused by her touch ran through his body and made Viktor shiver. He said his name, quietly, almost ashamed of the one strong word that he had never believed fit him, but Simone repeated it thoughtfully, kindly. She said, 'Well, I'll see you next week, Viktor,' and she let his hand go.

Viktor watched as Simone walked away swiftly, swaying slightly, wondering how those skinny legs could support her, especially on the three-inch high heels she wore. When she had turned the corner and was no longer in view, Viktor looked down at his hands and he couldn't bring himself to move his right hand, not yet, because he could still feel where Simone had touched him, and where her silky fingers had lightly stroked him.

Another customer came and climbed into the chair, opening up his newspaper to read while his shoes were shined. Viktor stared at his shaking hands for another moment, but when the customer cleared his throat, Viktor picked up his brush and returned to work.

* * *

Simone came the next week, and the next, and then the next. Viktor found himself preparing for her shines. He washed his rags and brushes and bought fresh bottles of polish and paste and rounds of wax and oil, to replace the old, partially full ones, and he dusted the chair his customers sat on and the low bench where they rested their feet, and he felt proud of his clean, organized shoe shine stand.

When she sat in his chair, he was careful not to look too closely at her legs, stretched out temptingly in front of him, or her face, friendly and long and sweet, with brown eyes wide and lovely. He made himself concentrate on the work and when she spoke to him, commenting on the weather or the latest news, he mumbled a response, relieved when she spoke again, in her rich, confident voice. Sometimes, she gave a little monologue, remarking on unimportant topics, and he enjoyed listening to her, nodding in confirmation. Mostly, Viktor was happy to watch Simone walking in the train station, coming and going from his stand in her secure and enthusiastic way, and he was happy to think about her later, when he was alone in his apartment, this thin, delicate, pretty brunette who proved his friends wrong. He wondered sometimes about who she really was; he only knew which train she came downtown on every morning and what sort of shoes she wore – usually pumps with pinched toes and overly high heels, dangerous shoes he wished he could warn her about – and which direction she went in after she left the station and how she adored her father, whom she had mentioned several times already. But even though Viktor was curious about what sort of job she had or where she lived or how she spent her evenings, he also didn't want to know those things. He didn't want to ruin his distant admiration for Simone by learning more about her.

On weekends at the bar or at someone's house, he listened to the guys talk about their wives as usual, and he wanted to speak up and tell them about Simone, about how fragile and yet robust she was, and about how she sat down in his chair every week as secure as any man, unashamed of letting him bend over her narrow feet to shine her shoes. He liked that Simone cared about her appearance and that she wanted to have the kind of special treatment most women didn't seem to think they deserved and Viktor thought he should share his new knowledge of women with his friends, and yet he couldn't. He wanted them to know how wrong they were, but he just sat there, unable to say anything. 'Women pay lots of attention at the top,' one guy explained, his voice disapproving, 'but the further down you get, the less they care. That's why they always walk around with scuffed shoes.' Another said, 'Instead of taking care of the shoes they've got, women just go out and buy another pair.' Viktor thought about Simone and imagined introducing her to his friends. He thought they would admire her and would stare boldly into her smiling but closed face before letting their gaze move downwards, ending at the high-heeled shoes as shiny as diamonds.

* * *

On a rainy early morning, Simone came towards his stand, holding her leather purse in one hand, a full plastic bag in the other. The bag hit against her legs as she walked, but Simone didn't seem to notice. She sat heavily down in the chair and sighed. 'I hate when it pours,' she said. 'I find rain so depressing.' She pushed her dark hair away from her eyes.

Viktor wanted to say or do something to make Simone smile, to take away the sad frown on her face, which wrinkled her forehead so that it looked like the creased leather on Viktor's oxfords, which he'd worn for more than twenty years. He started brushing away the dirt from her chocolate-colored pumps, and he tried to find the right words, but nothing came to him. He was relieved when Simone said, 'I have a request for you, Viktor.'

He took the cover off a black tin and covered one corner of a soft towel with wax. 'Oh? What is it?' He started to rub the wax over Simone's shoes, patterned like snakeskin.

She rattled the plastic bag in her lap and chuckled. 'I have a pair of shoes that are really a mess and I thought if anyone could make them look better, you could.'

Viktor looked up when she pulled the shoes out of the bag. The leather was black, but scuffed and dirty and rumpled and stretched and misshapen. Viktor put his towel across his thigh and reached for a shoe. He turned it over and looked at the sole, which was worn down to the fine nails that held it to the body. He wondered what Simone expected from him.

She said, her voice higher than usual, 'I hardly ever wear them, you know, not in years. But I've always liked them and wish I could wear them again.'

Viktor handed the shoe back to her and returned to work on the pair she was wearing. 'I'm not a shoe repair man,' he said, wishing he'd spoken more gently.

Simone said hurriedly, 'I know that. Yes, of course I do. I know you couldn't fix it all. But you do wonders with my shoes every week, Viktor, and I wish you would try.'

He buffed her shoes. 'It's rainy,' he said, just to say something in response.

'Naturally I'd pay you,' she said, ignoring his last useless comment.

Viktor was offended. Those shoes were old and ruined and not that much could be done for them. It wasn't a matter of money for him, but rather of pride in his work. He stood, feeling his knees creak as he pushed off the ground, and he realized with surprise how anxious and eager Simone looked. She held one shoe over each hand, as though they were gloves, and she was shaking her hands so that the shoes danced. She raised an eyebrow at him and smiled, her shoes waltzing in the air. Viktor paused, watching her, but then he let himself laugh and he nodded, reaching for the shoes.

'Thank you, Viktor,' Simone said, sounding like a delighted child. She pulled a small folded pile of money from her purse. Viktor would have liked to refuse her generous tip, but he didn't know how to do this, so he accepted the money, shoving the bills into his pocket as though he didn't care about them.

As she walked away, her newly shiny pumps clicking across the scraped and dusty marble floor, Viktor wondered how he could ever shine these shoes, and he watched with a sharp, nearly unbearable sadness as Simone disappeared through the doors of the train station.

* * *

It takes him hours that rainy night, but finally Viktor is satisfied. He has scrubbed away the dirt and massaged away the wrinkles and straightened the backs where they had folded over. He has polished the shoes to a glossy new black and covered them in protective layers of mink oil and buffed them until he can almost see his own reflection. He has ignored the aching of strain in his arms and back and wondered, with excitement and dread and hope, what Simone will say when she sees how unrecognizably beautiful he has made her shoes.

Viktor takes a chamois towel and runs it carefully over the shoes one last time, making sure that they are perfect. He puts away his tools, looks at Simone's shoes, and sighs, exhausted. The shoes are ready for her now; they are fixed and shined and it is Viktor who has made them look so new. He is proud of the job he has completed and he goes to bed, thinking only of Simone and her shiny shoes.

ESSAY

FOSSIL POETRY

Alan Wall

The year is 1811; the place Lyme Regis. A young woman called Mary Anning finds a skeleton that does not correspond to any form of life she has previously encountered. It is (or was) an ichthyosaurus, a name not yet available for her to utter. The name will need to be invented by bringing together syllables from a language in a form no longer spoken by the living. A long-dead creature will be reconstructed in its skeletal form and then described using a dead language. The Greek forms for fish and lizard will be brought together. If this is science's disturbed graveyard, it is also language's. While the ichthyosaurus lived, there was no such word as *ichthyosaurus*, and in any case no tongue to utter such a word.

Fossils, once discovered and described, resurrect a wordless past into a second life of meaning, and whenever we look into words we are also staring back into history. Take the word 'fossil': it originally meant simply something dug up, so there was no distinction between a brilliant mineral and a petrified form of organic life. This sense of digging is retained in that other word *fosse*, signifying a ditch or trench, and might even have survived in the Australian word *fossicking*, meaning to dig about or rummage in an unwelcome manner. In Emperor Rudolf II's

Wunderkammer, such items were displayed as freaks of nature, objects fashioned by the left hand of God, or shaped by what came to be known as the earth's own 'plastyck virtue'. Centuries later the word fossil will be specified, narrowed down so it referred only to the remains of once-living plants and creatures, now ossified.

By the time Mary Anning was hunting out her remains under the cliffs at Lyme Regis, the word fossil had become the centre of a manifold scientific endeavour, which would produce first Lyell, then Darwin. The fossils announced an age for the earth not previously considered possible. They also bespoke the extinction of species, which presented certain challenges to conventional assumptions about the nature of creation and the amount of time that had elapsed since that mighty inauguration detailed in the Book of Genesis. The fossils once re-assembled and considered spoke of evolution and mutation, and they also suggested that the earth was a very old place indeed, which had in its time seen entire species come and go.

The earth, once so confidently dated at around six thousand years, is now thought to be approximately four and a half billion years old. The harder we have stared at our planet, the older it has become. Bishop Ussher, after all, was walking around on the same crust and counting backwards from the genealogies in the Bible. The original moment of creation has also receded to an astounding 13.7 billion years. And what happened before that? There is no 'before that' about which to speculate. Our fossils have thus been situated in a changing intellectual world, and have in their turn helped to change that world.

The equivalent of palaeontology in language studies is etymology: the study of the origins of words. Language, said Emerson, is fossil poetry. And we should note something immediately about the state of any language: it could all have been otherwise. *Fossil* could have continued to mean anything dug out of the ground. Why, after all, should it not have done? This is not a question of propriety, but rather of arbitrary shifts that become conventions. Fossil has a scientific sound to it now, but its nimbus of precision was arbitrarily awarded. The word *venatic* relates to hunting and derives from the Latin *venari*, to hunt. Until the seventeenth century the word venison, which clearly relates to it, meant any meat taken from a hunted animal: rabbit, hare, even boar. If we think about it, the earlier usage was more logical than our own, which relates solely to deer, but logic can never be applied to usage. Or to put the matter differently, usage implies its own logic. The meaning of a word, said Ludwig Wittgenstein, is its use in the language. And when Samuel Johnson wrote his Preface to his great *Dictionary* of 1755, he explained that he had at one point hoped to fix the language, but had realised in the course of his endeavours that this was not possible. You can no more fix a language than you can a river. The force of their movement is constitutive of their identity.

So etymology discovers the hidden history inside the word; this is the fossil poetry to which Emerson alludes. Sometimes it's easy: dandelion is the Englishing of *dents de lyon*, the teeth of the lion, the yellow spears around the corolla of the plant being analogous to the speared dentition inside the big cat's mouth. Similarly with daisy, the day's eye, which we can trace back to the year 1000. Other studies are subtler if just as interesting. The word *selig* in Chaucer means without sin or blemish, and in 'The Prioress's Tale' the martyred child is described, employing that word, as undeserving of anything but the company of saints. How we then evolved *selig* into our present *silly* might give us pause. Such 'progress' takes us through an enormous amount of history and cultural change.

Has it become part of the responsibility of the serious writer, and the serious reader, to exhibit the fossil poetry inherent in language? Obliviousness to the fossil poetry in language might be permitted in a politician, but not a writer. If the latter says *pitfall* then he or she needs to envisage a dark hole and broken bones, not merely the standard cliché which long ago lost its sensual (and sensuous) context.

The scientific rigour applied to the study of fossils was soon to be matched by the attention that began to be paid to words and the history of their formation. This attention achieved its greatest monument in the *New English Dictionary*, first published in full in 1928. This has now become the *OED*. Its ghost is always a welcome presence in any serious consideration of language.

CONTRIBUTORS

Malcolm Bennett keeps chickens and bees, and is frequently an embarrassment to his family. By way of a job, he studies zoonoses, the diseases that human animals get from non-human animals

B.J. Epstein teaches literature and translation at the University of East Anglia, and she is also a writer, editor, and Swedish-to-English translator. www.awaywithwords.se.

Gill Gregory's collection, *In Slow Woods*, is published by rufus books (2011) and her experimental memoir, *The Sound of Turquoise* (KUP, 2009/10), has received critical acclaim. Gill lives on the Clapham/Brixton borders and teaches in Central London.

Heather Jones is a retired librarian who continues to indulge her passion for reading with StokeReads (Stoke-on-Trent Libraries Get Into Reading Groups).

Gabriel Josipovici was born in Nice of Russo-Italian, Romano-Levantine parents and lived in Egypt from 1845 to 156, when he came to this country. He is the author of fifteen novels, three collections of stories, and eight critical books, as well as radio and stage plays.

Brigid Lowe Crawford studied English at Bangor and Oxford and worked at the University of Sheffield and Trinity College, Cambridge. She has published books about sympathy in the Victorian novel and brain training for babies. She is now a full-time mother and honorary fellow at Liverpool.

Ian McMillan was born in 1956 and has been a freelance writer/ performer /broadcaster since 1981. He presents *The Verb* on BBC Radio 3 every Friday night.

Kate Miller was selected for Best British Poetry 2011 (Salt). In 2008 she won the Edwin Morgan International Poetry Prize. Kate has recently completed her doctoral thesis (in Creative Writing) on three poets who walk by the sea.

Peter Nicholson, Australian poet and author, was born in Waverley, New South Wales. He was educated at Armidale Teachers College and Macquarie University. His latest publication is the novella *Hammerhead*. See peternicholson.com.au for details.

Anna Lawrence Pietroni was training as a prison governor when she started writing in earnest. Her first novel, *Ruby's Spoon*, was published in 2011 (Vintage). She lives in Birmingham, runs creative writing workshops and is working on two more novels.

Jan Reeves studied Fine Art at St Martins School of Art. She lives and works in South London.

Peter Robinson's new collection of poetry is *The Returning Sky* (Shearsman Books), a Poetry Book Society Recommendation, published in January 2012. His anthology, *A Mutual Friend: Poems for Charles Dickens* (Two Rivers Press and the English Association) appears in February 2012 for the novelist's two-hundredth anniversary.

Julie-ann Rowell's pamphlet, *Convergence*, was a Poetry Book Society choice. Her first collection, *Letters North*, was shortlisted for the Inaugural Michael Murphy Memorial Prize, 2011, for best first collection in Britain and Ireland. She teaches poetry classes in Bristol.

Gordon Scapens retired early from a frantic world of electronics to enjoy walking, playing guitar and singing, and of course writing. 750 poems published in a variety of magazines

Alan Wall is a novelist, short story writer, poet and essayist. His latest novel *Badmouth* will appear soon from Quartet Books. He is professor of Writing and Literature at the University of Chester.

Jeanette Winterson is a writer and novelist. Her novel *Oranges Are Not the Only Fruit* won the 1985 Whitbread Prize for a first Novel. Her latest book, *Why Be Happy When You Could Be Normal?* was published by Jonathan Cape in October 2011.

Distribution Information

Trade orders Contact Mark Chilver, Magazine Department, Central Books

email: mark@centralbooks.com
web: www.centralbooks.com
tel: 0845 458 9925   fax: 0845 458 9912
Central Books, 99 Wallis Road, London, E9 5LN

All other queries regarding trade orders or institutional subscriptions
Contact The Reader Office

email: magazine@thereader.org.uk
tel: 0151 207 7207